THE EXPERT SUCCESS SOLUTION
——————— VOL. 2 ———————

A Deepak Chopra approach of tying sound scientific evidence with metaphysics and steps for us to experience it for ourselves. Katerina St. Clare offers insight and expert solutions for real!

> —**Tina Sacchi,** Bestselling Author of *My Spirit Is Not Religious: A Guide to Living YOUR Authentic Life*

As president of the Publishers Association of Los Angeles I've seen Steven Sanchez help people sort through the sea of choices confronting them. He has been sharing this amazing gift for more than 20 years. His no-nonsense, practical advice on how to narrow down the list and achieving success with the right choice for your business or your life is not to be missed. I see many books offering self-help advice. I am pleased to recommend the second installment of the bestselling Expert Success Solution. *His chapter is worth the price of the book alone.*

> —**Gary Young,** President, Publishers Association of Los Angeles

I'm honored to endorse Angela! I had the pleasure of writing the foreword for her autobiography, entitled Miracles in Action. *This action-packed chapter is just a sample of her book, which is a must-read! This chapter is simply a tease; you're going to want to know more about her incredible journey. What could have easily devastated her and her family forever now blesses all who hear this amazing story. She demonstrates with practical examples how you can turn your pain into power and grief into peace.*

> —**Eric Wilson,** *New York Times* bestselling author of *Fireproof* and *October Baby*, WilsonWriter.com

Pat's passion, knowledge and experience are some of the many qualities that make him successful and "Sell Yourself First (and Last!)" is a great motivational and inspirational invitation on how to live life with purpose, meaning and integrity. I have read and studied many resources about how to have more happiness and success in our lives for myself and my clients. This is the first in which I am motivated to implement not one or two but all seven steps, as Pat so eloquently wrote. You will not be disappointed if you are looking for a direct, easy and effortless way to achieve more and not work harder but smarter. Thank you, Pat, for leading the way!

> —**Anthony Diaz, JD,** The Divorce Empowerment Coach, www.anthonyjdiaz.com

This book is a must-read for anyone serious about creating the life they truly desire. Leslie Graham's chapter will motivate you to "Get Out of Your Own Way" to complete emotional and physical healing.

—**Bonnie Goldstone,** Stingray Hypnosis
Consultants International, StingrayHypnosis.com

Angela, in her relatively short life, has been faced with more than her share of incredible circumstances, any one of which could have changed her outlook on life. We have watched our niece not only endure but triumph over these challenges with a continuing positive attitude and an abiding trust in God. Indeed, it is her faith that has carried her through. By sharing her experiences . . . she provides encouragement and inspiration to all of us to rise above our losses and misfortunes and live our lives to the fullest.

—**Marilyn McCoo** and **Billy Davis Jr.,** Grammy award-winning
artists, formerly of The Fifth Dimension, McCooDavis.com

Making informed business and life choices becomes easier with Steven Sanchez's tips and suggestions. His system demystifies the process and his advice will help you, now and in the future.

—**Flo Selfman,** President, Independent Writers
of Southern California, IWOSC.org

Do you have several business ideas and projects you want to get started, but just don't know where to begin? Then you will love Rita Ferguson's chapter . . . Rita provides you with a strategic small business plan . . . guidelines for helping you to determine which project is right for your business and Rita steps for project planning as well. If you have ever found yourself overwhelmed and at a loss for where to begin with your business, or how to get your ideas and projects out of your head and implemented, then Rita's work is a must-read for you.

—**L. Nicholas, PhD,** The Financial Recovery Doctor

Rose Sheehan is an exceptional person, author, coach and leader. Words cannot sufficiently describe the value Rose has added to my life and business. Her chapter on "How to Be an Entrepreneur in a 9 to 5 Job" is a must-read for business owners and employees alike. Rose generously shares one of her business success exercises that is simple, practical, and actually works!

—**Mo Aronstein,** business owner

This book, and Pat Skiffington's chapter in particular, provides straightforward, no-nonsense ideas that will challenge your thinking and help you find your passion to keep driving toward success!

—**Craig Crossley, PhD,** Assistant Professor of Management, University of Central Florida, www.bus.ucf.edu/faculty/ccrossley

Would you seriously ignore advice from a nurse with 40 years' experience? I did not think so. I have witnessed Lesley Graham's abilities to reach out and touch the human race with a depth of compassion that brought tears to my eyes. She is a woman whose expertise I value without reservation. I trusted her with my own family.

—**Marie O'Riordan,** Success Developist™, Fortune 500 mentor, international honorary award-winning philanthropist, royal family's investments mentor, TheForeverMethod.com

Angela's "7 Steps from Grief to Peace" will help anyone seeking release from despair, hope in what seems hopeless, and the ability to feel love when love has been lost. As a former hospice chaplain, I applaud her courage to go deeper than her grief and find a bigger story to tell—a story that can transform lives. Her passion to help others is the peace that passeth all understanding.

—**M. Kris Landry, MRE,** author, speaker, singer/songwriter, counselor, and former hospice chaplain, TheStoryNeverEnds.com

Do you love your job? If you answered "NO" to this question without a slight hint of hesitation, then you need to read Rose Sheehan's chapter, "How to Be an Entrepreneur in a 9 to 5 Job." Rose helps you understand how you play a very important role, whether you are unemployed, self-employed, or work for someone else. Along with helping you to see yourself as an entrepreneur, Rose offers some wonderful exercises that you can do on the spot to help you create the ideal environment for yourself. She also provides you with ideas of how to position yourself to be successful. If you have been uncertain as to how to create the type of work you want to do, then this is the chapter for you. Let Rose help you to develop a blueprint that will LAUNCH your success.

—**Lorie Nicholas,** www.TheFinancialRecoveryDoctor.com

The Expert Success Solution, Volume 2 weaves in heartfelt stories with practical wisdom. With exemplary resiliency, Angela Alexander beautifully exemplifies the vital bond between feeling powerless and gaining resiliency. Angela gives us the steps that will provide new strength in not allowing our life-disrupting experiences to overtake us.

—**Lupe-Rebeka Samaniego, PhD**, clinical psychologist, speaker, bestselling collaborating author, *The Expert Success Solution, Volume 1*

The Expert Success Solution, Volume 2 will inspire and empower you to lead a richer and more fulfilling life. It is an essential read for those individuals who are sincerely interested in personal growth and reaching their true potential.

—**Chris Kent,** founder of Personal Liberation, PersonalLiberation.com

Barbara Cookson skillfully weaves personal experience and her work with clients to clearly describe life as a circle depicting the quality of our health and well-being. She uses specific examples and strategies to show readers a clear pathway to make seemingly impossible life-changing goals achievable . . . a must-read!

—**Jan Kristo, PhD,** professor, University of Maine, author of *Non-Fiction in Focus*

Barbara Cookson offers practical, easy-to-apply suggestions to turn your life around and empower yourself! Although she cites research to back up many of her techniques, her life is evidence of living into a lighter and happier you!

—**Rosalie Deer-Heart,** author, speaker, retreat leader, Heart-Soul-Healing.com

Barbara's steps to living a happy and healthy life offer simple but challenging ways for us to engage in choosing the lives we want to live.

Her hands-on approach encourages self-reflection and embraces her belief that with a little direction, we can live the lives we envision.

—**M. Kris Landry, MRE,** author, speaker, singer-songwriter, counselor, and former hospice chaplain, TheStoryNeverEnds.com

Marilyn Horowitz's guidance for her readers in "The Formative Event" is a rich mixture of the psychological, the spiritual, and the practical. She addresses non-writers, and welcomes them into the terrain of processing one's thoughts and feelings through writing. She goes further, however, in inspiring everyone to become a storyteller . . . She helps those who have not used or enjoyed writing to discover how to heal themselves through writing down their own personal stories and problems . . . to sorting out one's current life through writing out "the story" . . . offering some inspiring memories for us all!

—**Dr. Susan Kavaler-Adler,** psychologist, psychoanalyst, and author of *The Compulsion to Create: Women Writers and Their Demon Lovers,* KavalerAdler.com

Rose Sheehan is insightful, informative and practical. Her willingness to share knowledge is a huge advantage to her readers and business coaching clients. Knowledge is power! What better way for an entrepreneur, a business startup, a struggling business or, simply an owner ready to move to the next level and increase the odds of their success by reading her materials.

—**WL Laney,** #1 international bestselling author, radio host, and entrepreneur

The Expert Success Solution, Volume 2 is filled with captivating, page-turning advice. In a moving autobiographical journey, Lesley Anne Graham shares how to literally "climb out of bed" when faced with life-threatening illness. She combines mind-body-spirit with meaningful action while resonating deeply with the importance of sustaining an empathic healing connection.

—**Lupe-Rebeka Samaniego, PhD,** clinical psychologist, bestselling collaborating author of *The Expert Success Solution, Volume 1,* bestselling co-author of *The Winning Way,* speaker, Certified High Performance Coach

I am happy to endorse The Expert Success Solution, Volume 2. *Barry Laub, one of the collaborators of this book, has been a coach and a friend for almost 10 years. The thing I love most about his method is how well Barry understands that my professional life is really a reflection of my personal life. His three guiding principles—Attitude, Mindset, and Purpose—have transformed both. Knowing his commitment to making a difference for everybody he meets, and the quality of authors in this book compels me to urge everyone to seriously read the words of wisdom in this masterful book.*

—**Dr. Fred Blum,** EnergyRichLiving.com

I urge anyone suffering from chronic illness to read RN Lesley Graham's chapter, where she offers five simple but powerful steps to help individuals take charge of their own health and recover from chronic diseases such as heart disease, autoimmune disease, and diabetes. With over 40 years of experience as a registered nurse trained in traditional medicine, Lesley was forced to look outside the box, taking an active role in her own recovery from Lyme disease. She now offers her discovery to others facing chronic illness in this enlightening chapter.

—**Babs Kangas, PhD, c**o-author of the #1 international bestseller,
The Expert Success Solution, FreeFunAndFabulous.com

Professor Marilyn Horowitz work will transform your life from where it is now to where you want it to be tomorrow. The process and the tools she offers are not only exceptional but also totally workable in your life. Marilyn looks at the entire picture, from inside out and outside in. She is an expert in examining the situation with understanding, knowledge, experience and wisdom and ultimately she filters the need with outstanding passion and success. The materials and the exercises Marilyn presents in The Expert Success Solution *will help you and teach you gently to move forward and shift from the ordinary to the extraordinary.*

—**Ana Weber,** bestselling author,
financial turnaround expert, business life coach

This is a book which is easy to read, yet chock full of transformative information. I am pleased to give it my seal of approval as a self-help book that is a game changer. I have been reading and studying the gurus in the industry for over 25 years. This collaboration of impressive authors has put together a collection of wisdom that can hold its own with most any other book out there. Read it, learn and grow.

—**Rich Fasano,** investment banking executive

Marilyn Horowitz never ceases to astonish me. With the Formative Event Exercise, she once again leads us on a new creative journey, this one to not only deepen our writing but to expand our understanding of our inner selves.

—**Adam Nadler,** assistant copy editor, *Vanity Fair*

Having been a nurse for 40 years Lesley has deep understanding of healing the body, mind, and spirit. The core of her message speaks to the story one holds in his/her body. She takes us beyond the diagnosis and introduces steps that empower us to recognize that we are in charge of our own well-being and can activate the healing mechanism within.

—**M. Kris Landry, MRE,** author, speaker, singer-songwriter, counselor, and former hospice chaplain, TheStoryNeverEnds.com

Marilyn Horowitz's timed writing exercise forced me to listen to my intuition and reconnect with memories I never even realized mattered. I think I achieved in 15 minutes what might have taken many long hours in therapy.

—**Kate Novack,** producer, *Page One: Inside the New York Times, Ivory Tower,* and *Le Cirque: A Table in Heaven*

Pat did a fabulous job on this chapter regarding how to overcome failure and the challenges of selling. This is a must-read for anyone wanting to master the Seven Core Pillars of Sales Success. One simply has to fail faster to succeed sooner!

—**Dr. Cheryl Lentz,** The Academic Entrepreneur™, ThinkingBeyondLimits.com

Lesley Graham is a truly inspirational woman, a person I have listened to and firsthand seen the benefits in my own life . . . I am now happier, more positive, driven, motivated and content than I have ever been in my life and it's only been one month since I read her story. This is the power of the mind and the universe when we change the way we think.

—**Elys G. N. Poppy,** founder of Eclectic magazine

Professor Horowitz brilliantly reminds us that "the stories are within us." Her daily writing activity is a simple and reflective tool for dealing with daily challenges and conditioned behaviors that keep us stuck in life. Both writers and non-writers can benefit from suggestions and insights offered in this powerful chapter. The path to inner peace is enriched when we dance with the pen.

—**Dr. Connie Hebert,** education entrepreneur, author of The Teachable Minute: The Secret to Raising Smart and Appreciative Kids, ConnieHebert.com

Everyone looking for a practical, how-to, step-by-step guide to improve not only your personal but also your professional life must-read The Expert Success Solution, Volume 2. It is treasure trove for everyone interested in connecting with who you are and where you want to be. Ann Van De Water's chapter is a perfect example. She is passionate about stress-less parenting and offers a step-by-step method to help you accomplish this.

—**BJ Rosenfeld,** creator of the CD series 5 Secrets to an Enviable Relationship for Parents and Adult Children, BJRosenfeld.com

Echoed within the pages of this book are the stepping stones to success: challenge, choice, courage, creativity and commitment—regardless of the situation. Lesley Graham demonstrates each of these in her journey back from a ticking time bomb of a tick bite which robbed her of her physical health and mental acuity. Choosing to stand up and take charge, Lesley courageously sought solutions outside the "no can do" attitude offered by mainstream medicine, regaining her health and vitality. This 5-Point Plan throws a lifeline to anyone with chronic illness or fatigue, inviting you to change your relationship with your illness and embrace life once more.

—**Janet Swift,** #1 international bestselling author, LifeChangingCafe.com

I've never had any children—that is, until my mom moved in with memory issues. Reading Ann Van De Water's chapter made me realize that I could use her steps to smooth out my relationship with my mom, who

has essentially become my child in so many ways. I will be taking what I learned into all the relationships I have, not just parent-child!

—**Laura Steward (Atchison),** expert in embracing
the feminine wisdom of entrepreneurship,
host of *Entrepreneur Master Class* radio show

Professor Marilyn Horowitz will change the way you write and live your life. Even if you are not a writer, the bonus for everyone who ever puts pen to paper is that it will change your perspective on how you view the world. Her Formative Event exercise that she presents in The Expert Success Solution *is a technique well worth learning, helping anyone grow in their business and in their life.*

—**Anne Kleinman**

I recommend that parents read and follow Ann Van De Water's practical, step-by-step advice for (re)building a loving connection with their kids via respect, communication and personal responsibility. Ann's sage advice is in great company with other experts in this terrific book who collaborated to bring us important lessons for business and life.

—**Jennifer A. Rosenwald,** co-author, #1 international bestseller
The Expert Success Solution, JenniferRosenwald.com

Ann's searing insight into the combustible world of raising a young adult offers six steps that help untangle the emotional and psychological mine field between a parent and child. Acknowledging and honoring each other's feelings is at the core of Ann's important work, and as a former hospice chaplain, I support her approach to get to the "real" story before it's too late.

—**M. Kris Landry, MRE,** author, speaker, singer/songwriter,
counselor, and former hospice chaplain, TheStoryNeverEnds.com

Parenting experts Ann Van De Water and Lorraine Pursell offer positive and effective solutions for coping with behaviors that "push our buttons" as parents. Readers will benefit from Ann's Six Steps to Stress-Less Parenting as well as Lorraine's 4-F Formula for converting parenting mistakes into loving engagement with children on a daily basis. These simple and easy solutions are based on real-life experiences and professional expertise that can help even the most frustrated parent to move forward on the path to peaceful parenting.

—**Dr. Connie Hebert,** education entrepreneur, author of
*The Teachable Minute: The Secret to Raising Smart
and Appreciative Kids,* ConnieHebert.com

Barry Laub has a passion for helping others be all that they could be. His chapter demonstrates the steps needed to guide professionals to uncover their passion and live a life with purpose. Barry's wisdom shines through in his chapter and anyone who reads it will benefit greatly. Barry is truly a master of mindset.

—**Tom Antion**

A MUST-read for all parents, Ann Van De Water's chapter provides valuable and practical tips for surviving the most difficult parenting years. Ann also serves as an inspiration to many previous full-time parents to follow their passion and reinvent themselves after their children are grown.

—**Babs Kangas**, **PhD,** co-author, #1 international bestseller *The Expert Success Solution,* and founder of FreeFunandFabulous.com

The Expert Success Solution, Volume 2 *offers the keys to stepping into the life you have always desired but did not know where or how to begin. With simple yet powerful clarity, Ann Van De Water guides you into the steps needed to maintain a meaningful relationship with children of any age and demonstrates beautifully how to reconnect with your adolescent when your relationship has been ruptured. A must-read!*

—**Lupe-Rebeka Samaniego, PhD,** clinical psychologist, bestselling
collaborating author of *The Expert Success Solution, Volume 1,*
bestselling co-author of *The Winning Way,*
speaker, Certified High Performance Coach

As a hypnotherapist and Reiki master/practitioner, I am in complete agreement with Katerina St. Claire! We all hold the incredible power and ability to heal ourselves. I know that you will enjoy Katerina's viewpoint from a proven scientific aspect. You won't want to miss Katerina's "5 Steps

to Feeling Your Own Energy Force," which will help you connect with universal energy to heal yourself emotionally and physically.

—**Bonnie Goldstone,** Stingray Hypnosis Consultants International, StingrayHypnosis.com

Lesley's story is as inspiring as her journey has been to witness over the last several years. Her courage with us in Peru made it clear that she is on a mission to awaken personally and bring that information to the world. The world is a better place with Lesley in it to be sure, and I know that Heaven on Earth will expand for anyone that heeds her words.

—**Jennifer Hough,** bestselling author, speaker, and founder of TheWideAwakening.com

Angela Alexander is a woman of substance and has my highest recommendation. Her impact is truly immeasurable. Even while hearing her phenomenal story the producer in me was already visualizing the scenes and knew her book was movie worthy. My team immediately requested to produce Miracles in Action—The Documentary! *The film is currently in production; we are extremely excited for the first screening, the red carpet premiere, and more importantly for you to search for and share your* Miracles in Action.

—**Evan Money,** bestselling author, global entrepreneur, and executive producer of *Words of Art*, starring Joel Osteen, Darren Hardy, Mark Batterson, and Zig Ziglar, TakeActionProductions.com

Barry Laub has amazing authenticity and an amazing sense of self. If you want to learn how to lead a life of fulfillment, listen to Barry and let him guide you to your purpose.

—**Peggy McColl,** *New York Times* Bestselling Author

THE

EXPERT
SUCCESS
SOLUTION

—— VOL. 2 ——

*Get Solid Results
in 16 Areas of Business and Life*

WENDY LIPTON-DIBNER
and RICK FRISHMAN

with 14 LEADING EXPERTS

NEW YORK

THE EXPERT SUCCESS SOLUTION Vol. 2
Get Solid Results in 16 Areas of Business and Life

Published in New York, New York, by Morgan James Publishing. Morgan James and The Entrepreneurial Publisher are trademarks of Morgan James, LLC. www.MorganJamesPublishing.com

The Morgan James Speakers Group can bring authors to your live event. For more information or to book an event visit The Morgan James Speakers Group at www.TheMorganJamesSpeakersGroup.com.

A **free** eBook edition is available with the purchase of this print book.

CLEARLY PRINT YOUR NAME ABOVE IN UPPER CASE

Instructions to claim your free eBook edition:
1. Download the BitLit app for Android or iOS
2. Write your name in **UPPER CASE** on the line
3. Use the BitLit app to submit a photo
4. Download your eBook to any device

ISBN 978-1-63047-489-8 paperback
ISBN 978-1-63047-490-4 eBook
Library of Congress Control Number:
2014919745

Cover Design by:
Rachel Lopez
www.r2cdesign.com

Interior Design by:
Bonnie Bushman
bonnie@caboodlegraphics.com

In an effort to support local communities, raise awareness and funds, Morgan James Publishing donates a percentage of all book sales for the life of each book to Habitat for Humanity Peninsula and Greater Williamsburg.

Get involved today, visit
www.MorganJamesBuilds.com.

Habitat for Humanity®
Peninsula and
Greater Williamsburg
Building Partner

This book is dedicated to all who are willing to put their egos aside in search of collaborative solutions to the challenges we face worldwide.

CONTENTS

PREFACE

Welcome to *The Expert Success Solution, Volume 2*. The book you hold in your hands is the result of a carefully crafted collaboration of 16 experts in personal and professional development.

This book took 12 months to create and was a true labor of love for all of us.

If you read *The Expert Success Solution, Volume 1*, you know that book represented the first time 22 independent experts from entirely different industries sat in a room together to bring you a solid solution for your business and your life in a simple and entertaining book.

The response to Volume 1 was overwhelmingly positive. We were honored to hit number one on the international bestseller list less than 12 hours after we released the book to the world, and the feedback was truly humbling.

Our readers loved Volume 1 so much that we decided to do it again!

And here we are, bringing you a second collaborative solution to help you get more from your business and your life.

Unlike movie sequels that rarely continue the greatness of a brand, *The Expert Success Solution, Volume 2* lives up to its name and its promise.

Our 16 collaborating authors met for four days in a retreat setting where they worked long hours to find their unique contributions to this book. Through that process, they learned more about themselves and each other than they ever imagined was there and discovered the true meaning of the word "synergy."

Since then we have held monthly meetings, connected virtually and in person, and continued coordinating our efforts to bring you this collaborative solution.

A tremendous amount of personal experience and professional expertise is contained within the pages of this book, and we hope it will serve you well in your business and your life.

In 16 strategically crafted and lovingly created chapters, you'll discover proven solutions for starting and/or growing any business with steps you can use to achieve your business goals faster.

You'll discover secrets to ensure your business is the right fit for you and that you get projects accomplished, never sell yourself short, always make great choices, select a business and life that's perfect for you, and never settle for second best.

Of course, business thrives only when we're balanced in our personal life. So you'll find time-tested advice for parenting that is street-smart and savvy so you can give yourself a break for being human. You'll get questions you can ask to find your life purpose and questions you can ask to make great choices in business and life.

You'll get wonderful tips to help you heal from illness, injury, chronic pain, and devastating loss so you can live a happy and healthy life in a body that will serve you well.

With so much advice, how do you know where to begin? Well, here's a little preliminary advice to help you *use* all you'll receive in the chapters to follow.

How to Get the Most from
The Expert Success Solution, Volume 2

As in Volume 1, this book is strategically designed to give you step-by-step, practical strategies you can use to create greater success in every area of your life.

We invite you to refrain from deciding whether a chapter fits your needs simply by its title.

Read each chapter—even if it doesn't seem to be a fit. There is wisdom you can glean and practical tips you can learn in every chapter you'll read, all of which will apply to areas of your life that may not be obvious at first.

The chapters in this book are purposefully short so you can grab just what you need and move to the next. Start by taking these two steps:

Step 1: Take Stock

Before you begin reading, answer the two questions below by making a list in the left-hand column of each chart (ignore the second column for now).

1. How would you like things to be different in your business life?

Make your list here and be specific!	Chapter(s)

2. How would you like things to be different in your personal life (family, friends, personal health, and well-being)?

Make your list here and be specific!	Chapter(s)

Step 2: Connect Each Chapter

After you read each chapter, come back to these pages, review your two lists, **and write the number of the chapter you just completed next to each item that was addressed for you by that chapter.**

Step 3: Implement!

Once you've finished reading the book, come back to your list and implement the advice you received in the associated chapter(s) you've listed, one item at a time, one chapter at a time, one set of steps at a time. Then, when you're ready . . .

Come Celebrate with Us!

As you complete each chapter, join us on our Facebook page (search *The Expert Success Solution*) and we'll celebrate with you!

If you have any questions along the way, join us there and we will all be accessible to you—all there for you and ready to help!

It is our sincere hope that our collaboration will bring you more success in every area of your life and that you will share this book with people you love, because true success comes when you help others.

Thank you for permitting us the honor of serving you!

—Wendy, Rick, Pat, Helena, Steven, Rita, Barb, Marilyn, Joyce, Ann, Lorraine, Angela, Barry, Lesley, Katerina, and Rose

1

FOCUS ON IMPACT™

Wendy Lipton-Dibner, MA

"How can I get traffic to my website?"
"How can I grow my email list?"
"How can I get people to open and read my emails?"
"How can I get people to like, engage with, and share my posts?"
"How can I get people to buy my products and services?"
"How can I make money fast?" and
"How can I love my life along the way?"

D o these questions sound familiar to you? If so, good for you! These are the exact questions I get from leading influencers around the globe, so you're in great company.

What's really fascinating about these 7 questions is that business owners have been asking me the *same* questions for over 3 decades. Of course, 30 years ago, the *language* was a bit different:

*"How can I get traffic to my **business**?"*
*"How can I grow my **mailing** list?"*
*"How can I get people to open and read **my letters**?"*
*"How can I get people to **read** and **respond to** my **advertising**?"*
*"How can I get people to buy **what I sell**?"*
"How can I make money fast?" and
"How can I love my life along the way?"

And here's what's even more amazing:

The answer I gave clients in 1983 is exactly the same response I give my clients today but the *results* they're getting in this difficult economy are even stronger than we saw during the flush economy of the '80s!

One simple, time-tested strategy has brought success on all 7 business issues in every industry you can imagine, during some of the worst economic conditions of the past 100 years.

Wow.

So what is this magic strategy?

FOCUS ON IMPACT. ™

"That's one of those touchy-feely things, right?"

No. This is proven strategy and smart business.

From branding to marketing to list growing to product delivery to customer service to repeat and referral sales, the shortest distance between where you are and where you want to be is to *focus on impact.*

I've celebrated with entrepreneurs, doctors, nonprofit directors, top influencers, and Fortune 100 CEOs as they cried tears of joy and relief from the mind-boggling results they'd created—all with this one strategy.[1]

So how do you make it happen? First, understand the foundation that drives the process:

When you *focus on impact,* everything shifts in response— starting with you. Instead of lying awake at night worrying about

---

1 Survey research revealed increased revenues by as much as 200% in fewer than 30 days in companies that shifted their business focus to impact and implemented the steps in this chapter.

money, your thoughts turn to how you can make a greater difference in the world.

This service-oriented thinking alters your brain chemistry so you wake up each morning filled with pride, excitement, and increased energy.

Your mind develops heightened creativity as you discover all-new avenues to grow your impact.

The more you focus on impact, the more you'll meet like-minded people who will want to partner with you.

Here's an example:

The first day I met my fabulous co-author Rick Frishman, we introduced ourselves and then—simultaneously—asked, *"So how I can help you?"*

We burst out laughing and have been dear friends and partners ever since. We each have separate businesses, but we partner and support each other year-round because we share an extraordinary desire to impact people's lives and always have that as our primary focus.[2]

When you focus on impact, you'll start initiating impact-driven conversations with people you meet and discover a network of supporters you never imagined possible.

You'll have new conversations with your market and grow a community of people who want—and will pay premium fees for—the impact they'll get as a result of using your products and services.

Your business will grow exponentially in response because,

When you focus on impact, the money will come™.

The only thing that will stall or stop your growth is if you lose sight of your focus on impact.

So how can you capitalize on this strategy—particularly in a global climate that's defined by cynicism, skepticism, and cautious-spendingism?[3] Start here:

---

2   See Rick Frishman's chapter 2 and discover what's possible when you come from a giving place. Hint: You get to work from your pool!

3   No, that's not a word. But don't you think it should be?

3 Steps to Grow Your Influence and Income as a Result of Your Impact

Step 1: Stop Thinking about Money

By definition, business is about generating profits: measure ROI, check your accounts daily, celebrate when sales come in and panic when sales are down, buy more advertising, get a bigger footprint, focus on competition, and *never* take your eye off the bottom line.

This is normal business practice, but just because it's normal doesn't make it smart. It's normal for a baby to try to stick his finger in an electrical outlet. That doesn't make it smart.

Do you want to sell your products and services? Stop thinking about money and *focus on impact.*

Do want to increase your social rankings? Stop thinking about money and *focus on impact.*

Do you want to make so much money you don't have to think about money? Stop thinking about money *NOW* and *focus on impact.*

Here's the truth they don't teach in business school:

> **Serious money comes when you stop focusing on money and turn all your attention to making a lasting impact on every life you touch.**

Every time you find yourself thinking about making money, STOP and ask yourself one question:

How can I make an impact right now that will help people get what they truly want?

Step 2: Define Your Impact

Here's a question for you:

How would giving you my money get me closer to something I want—something that has nothing to do with what you sell?

Before you answer, tread carefully lest you fall into one of the most dangerous of all business traps: *Business Ignorance*. This is what happens when we assume we know what people really want and conduct business according to our assumptions. We move to the Dark Side, where people are nothing more than faceless cash generators.

I strive every day to avoid the Dark Side. I'm guessing you're with me on this or you would have stopped reading by now.

So if impact is about helping people get closer to what they want, then how do you find out what they truly want so you can define how you can best make your impact?

You invite your market to do it for you.

In graduate school I had the privilege of studying under some of the greatest social researchers in history. They instilled in me a neurotic need to go straight to the source and to never assume the truth without testing it.

Their advice has served me well in building 10 successful businesses. It also turned me into a research snob.

I invite you to join me in this elite club. It will help you serve *more* people *more* of what you've got and get *more* rewards for the impact you bring to their lives through your products and services.

The process is simple: **SPY-SURVEY-STRATEGIZE**.

1. **SPY:** Read the blogs of your target market(s), visit their social sites, and attend their conferences. Note the words they use to describe their dreams and their struggles.
2. **SURVEY:** Send emails, use online questionnaires, and literally pick up the phone (*gasp!*) to talk with them. Ask questions to determine what they really want beyond your products and services.
3. **STRATEGIZE:** Once you have a clear list of everything your community wants, reverse-engineer each item to identify specifically what they would (logically) have to do, be, and have so they would be able to achieve each item. Dig deep— your entire life is filled with experiences that will give you

the answers you seek. When your list is done, you'll be ready for Step 3.

Step 3: Use Impact-Driven Content Marketing™

Traditional marketing is about raising brand awareness through product-related advertising. While there is plenty of advertising in today's economy, the digital age has now opened up an unprecedented opportunity for us to move away from old (and expensive) marketing techniques and segue into a powerfully effective, low-cost strategy I call Impact-Driven Content Marketing™ (IDCM).

So what is IDCM? It's YOU providing practical, actionable, and targeted information in an easy-to-access format across multiple platforms that will help us in our lives over and over and over again.

But who would care what I think? Who would listen to me?

Somewhere out there, someone is waiting to hear *your* voice, read *your* post, and feel *your* compassion. That person is waiting for information only *you* can provide—information you use every day and have long since taken for granted. When you discover that one person who needs you, that person will lead you to an entire community.

So how do I know what information they need?

Look back over your life at all you've overcome, all you've learned, all you've become. Each moment of your life contains a lesson you can use to make your impact and—as a result—grow your influence and income.

The secret to thriving in a down economy is:

Capitalize on tumultuous times by turning yourself (and, by extension, your company) into the go-to resource for how-to information relative to (but not about) your products and services.[4]

The more you help people, the more interested they will become in everything you offer. It's that simple.

---

4   It amazes me more businesses haven't caught on to this, but right now you're on the right side of the tipping point to capitalize.

IDCM will help you grow your reach, establish global influence, create measurable impact, and ultimately increase revenues. How long it will take and how far you can go is entirely a function of how quickly and effectively you create and release your IDCM to your market.

Of course, the secret is to create IDCM that will actually create results for people so they will do what you teach and share it with everyone they know. Here's how:

- Take the list you created in Step 2, and for each item, create a simple, practical, how-to IDCM piece with actionable steps people can do immediately.
- Serve up your tips LIVE through speaking engagements and in media interviews and VIRTUALLY through blogs, social media posts, short videos, webinars, teleseminars, and MP3 audios/podcasts. Offer all of this at no charge.
- Pay careful attention to what you say and how you say it. You don't have to be the world's greatest speaker or a bestselling author to be effective with IDCM, but it's critical to use language and presentation styles your community will connect with so they trust you quickly. You've got less than six seconds to win in our ADD world so use them wisely and remember: Connect Before Commerce™.
- In order to make your greatest impact, people need to implement your how-to advice. So brush up on ethical influence formulas that Move People to Action™ so people will trust you, do what you say, and get measurable results. That's when your impact will be felt deeply and shared virally.[5]

---

[5]   See my chapter in *The Expert Success Solution, Volume 1* for the 5 steps to Move People to Action™.

Start Now

If you're still asking the question *"How can I make money fast?"* just remember this:

We are all born with the amazing power to make an impact on people's lives, and life's greatest journey is to find our unique impact and make it happen before it's too late.

So forget about money and *focus on impact*. Walk the steps I've outlined for you here, one step at a time, until you've done them all and then smile at the impact you've made and the lifestyle you'll be living—this will be your reward for the difference you made in people's lives.

Start now. Because life is far too short to settle for less than you truly want—in your business or your life. And because the world needs your impact NOW.

WENDY LIPTON-DIBNER, MA, is a multiple-time bestselling author and internationally recognized authority on business acceleration through impact strategy. President of Professional Impact, Inc., and founder of *The Action Movement*™ and the *Move People to Action*™ system, Wendy is a trusted business advisor to doctors, executives, entrepreneurs, and top influencers worldwide. Learn more about Wendy in "Meet the Experts."

2

WORK FROM YOUR POOL

Rick Frishman

The business world can be challenging, discouraging, and scary—but it can also be inspiring, rewarding, and fulfilling. There will be ups and downs, like in any other profession. The key is that when we are down, we have to stay inspired and turn things around.

My journey in the business world has taught me a lot about myself and others. I started my own company, and I built it from the ground up. I have spent countless hours and expended tons of energy planning and pursuing my dreams. Yes, I have made mistakes along the way, but in doing so I've also learned invaluable life lessons—all of which made it possible for me to have had the opportunity to work with some of the greatest entrepreneurs in the world.

It's also enabled me to do what I want to do on my terms. And that means I get to work from my pool. Literally. I swim when I want to swim, play when I want to play, and work when I want to work.

Working from your pool doesn't have to mean you ever touch the water. It just means you learn how to work smart, not hard, so you have the freedom to do what you want, when you want. Here's how.

6 Steps to Work from Your Pool

Step 1: Feel the Temperature of the Water

After years of working in the corporate world, I have developed a sharp instinct about people and learned to trust my instincts when entering into any business deal.

Instinct is like having antennae that are constantly absorbing information and sending signals to the brain about how to proceed. Over time, my antennae have grown strong, and, as a result, I am great at figuring people out really fast. I can tell almost immediately if a person is going to be a good business partner or not.

Years ago, a major conglomerate wanted to buy my company. They had lawyers there and were ready for me to sign the papers and seal the deal. But my antennae were buzzing, so I said, *"I just need a few minutes. I've just got to think,"* and I walked away from the table.

I went outside to clear my head, came back about 20 minutes later, and said, *"You know what? It just doesn't feel right. I'm not going to do the deal."*

I turned down a multi-million-dollar deal because it didn't feel right. To this day, I know I made the right decision.

Always feel the temperature of the water and then go with your gut. If it doesn't feel right, don't jump in.

Step 2: Check the Rules of the Pool

Every pool has its own set of rules. Here's mine.

Any time you're making a business deal
only for the money, it's the wrong decision.

You've got to do it for more than the money, or you will always make the wrong choice. When you do it for the right reasons, you are growing your business with good people. They will want to help at least as much as they want the money.

I've had the experience of working with people who were only in it for the money and have vowed to never work with another company or person who only cares about the money. I made it my goal to only work for the right reasons.

You've got to decide what your right reasons are. For me, it was about getting what's right for myself and for my family.

So what are the rules of YOUR pool?

Step 3: Choose the Right Pool

Make it your goal to work with people who want to give back and with people who have the same values as you. For example, I was fortunate to meet David Hancock, the founder of Morgan James Publishing, several years ago at a seminar. We began talking and quickly figured out we had the same values.

One of the values we share is giving back. That's why at Morgan James Publishing, we give a portion of the proceeds from every book we publish to Habitat for Humanity.

One of the things I love about working with David is that he is always serving and giving back. Sure, he wants to make money, but that isn't his core reason for running Morgan James Publishing. He just loves going to work every day and helping folks—helping authors and building houses.[6]

---

6   David is the president of Habitat for Humanity for the Commonwealth of
     Virginia. This is a wonderful organization that builds houses for people in need.
     After we give them a house and put a roof over their heads, we give them a library
     of books because we also want to fill their heads with knowledge.

It is because of his ethics and values, and the fact that he has surrounded himself with others who share his values, that he is so successful in all his business endeavors.

When you choose the right pool, success will come.

Step 4: Jump in from the High Diving Board

Every entrepreneur I know talks about the risks in life. They say, "*You know what? I've made it, and then I haven't made it, and then I've made it again.*"

For example, take Donald Trump. He has been up $500 million and down $500 million but he always knew, no matter what, that when he was down he could come back do it again.

Success requires a belief that you are going to take a risk and succeed. Believe in yourself and bring in the right people to help you along the way.

Before taking a risk, make sure you have put away a bit of money to hold you over while you are in transition. While taking a risk can be worth it, don't do it if you aren't going to be able to pay your mortgage or pay for your kids' college. You need to be very realistic about how long you can sustain yourself and your family before you start making money again.

The number one thing to do when considering risks is an assessment of how much you can spend and save. If you have no savings and no money to put away, it isn't a good idea to leave your safe place just to try something new. Instead, take the time to save up some money so you will be prepared when you take the risk.

Harvey Mackay, who is one of my clients and dear friends, said, "*Dig your well before you're thirsty.*"

Start the process and dig your pool before you need it. Start digging now and get yourself together so that when you're ready to jump in from the high diving board, the risk will be lessened because you're jumping in prepared. Before you jump, do this:

3 Things You Must Do Before Taking a Risk

1. **Do an assessment.** Do a real assessment of how much money you have saved. Do you have six months, a year, two years put away? Think hard about how much time you will have to get your new business up and running, and making a profit.

2. **Build while you're still in business.** Build your new business while you still have your old. For example, before I started working at Morgan James and Author101 University, I was building my platform, education, lists, and website, and getting everything put together before I branched out on my own. Build it before you leave so you have a solid foundation to stand on.

3. **Line up your partners.** I don't believe anybody can do it alone. Figure out who is in your pool, and pick the people you know you can work with. Make a list of all your potential partners and then do some research. Choose people who have the same values as you and who you know will give back. Choose wisely.

Step 5: Utilizing Your Pool

This will be my 17th book, and not one of them was done alone. I have co-authors in every book I do.

Beginning in 1976, I had a wonderful partner in my business whom I could rely on. He was my mentor. It is important to really do your research on potential partners. You want to know the good and the bad. Find out everything wonderful and terrible about them and ask them, "*What were your biggest mistakes, and why aren't you making them anymore?*"

Make them identify their values and explain their business philosophy, and only work with them if their values match your own.

Pay attention to the strengths and weaknesses of potential partners. If you've both got the same strengths, then you only need one of you.

The ideal partnership is one in which the people are polar opposites in terms of strengths. For example, I am as ADD as they come, but my partner Wendy Lipton-Dibner makes long to-do lists before she even moves. Together, we make a wonderful partnership because we're different, but on important things, we come from the same place: the heart. We both want to help people and give back.[7]

By working with others, we allow ourselves even more opportunity to grow.

Step 6: Enjoy Your Pool

When I worked in corporate America, I traveled on the Long Island Expressway for an average of three hours a day. I did that for 35 years. You can do the math to see how much of my life was wasted commuting. I was living without the freedom to make many of my own decisions. This was one of the deciding factors when I chose to sell my company and take a risk on working from home.

Another factor was that I had hip replacement surgery, which required me to spend an entire summer doing rehab. To make things easier, I did it in my pool, and I ran my whole business from my pool at the same time. The freedom I experienced working from home was something I'd wanted all the time—I'd just never seen it until that summer.

Of course, you don't actually have to be in an actual *swimming* pool—find the metaphorical pool that you can enjoy. Work from your house, or in the mountains, or at the beach, or on an island in the Caribbean—the number one thing is to find your pool so you can enjoy the freedom. It's a wonderful thing.

When you work for yourself in your favorite pool, you call the shots and choose the people you want in the pool with you. This is important for living a healthy and fulfilling life. It means working with the people you want, for the people you want, and in your own manner.

---

7   See Wendy Lipton-Dibner's chapter 1 to see how giving back can get you everything you want!

The focus should be on the happiness factor in your life. If you're going to work every day and you're dreading it and you're not happy, you are not truly living. It's about waking up every day and feeling happy about what you're doing, how you're doing it, and with whom.

Dedicate more time to yourself and your family, and do the right thing for them. When you do that, you'll be working from your pool, doing it the way you want, and living the life you have always wanted.

What I want for you is to go out there, multiply, be happy, and spread the word that from this day forward, we're going to change the world and be happy campers along the way.

RICK FRISHMAN is a multiple-time bestselling author, publisher at Morgan James Publishing in New York, and founder of Planned Television Arts (now called Media Connect). He has been one of the leading book publicists in America for more than 35 years. Learn more about Rick in "Meet the Experts."

3

SELL YOURSELF FIRST (AND LAST!)

Pat Skiffington

t is noon on Wednesday, though it feels like 5 p.m. on Friday. Dave has never felt more stress related to a job as he does right now. The pressure to perform is intense—at work and home. He is way behind on his sales numbers and living off borrowed time. His sales manager is also feeling the pressure and, as much as he likes Dave, has given him 60 days to perform and catch up on his quotas or face the end of the road. Dave has not had the courage to break this news to his wife. Something has got to give.

Dave's story is all too common in the world of sales where failure is the norm. Research shows that salespeople who struggle with sales-call reluctance earn an average of 80% less in commission income than their counterparts who have conquered their fears—even if all other things are equal (talent, drive, motivation, intelligence, experience, etc.).[8]

If you hold one of the 87.7% of the jobs in the United States that *don't* involve full-time sales, you might be wondering,

Why am I reading a chapter about sales in a success book?

The answer is simple: We are ALL in sales. The better you are at selling and self-promotion, the more successful you'll be in your career and even at home.

Not everyone is meant to be a salesperson; however, we all need to understand how to promote ourselves (*sell* ourselves) when appropriate. When is it appropriate? Whenever we have something to give or share with others.

Think about it—we *sell* ourselves to our friends and co-workers when we are looking for a job (or promotion) and when we are single and looking for our soul mate (or while we wait to meet "the one"). We *sell* ourselves when we compete in anything; we *sell* ourselves on social media hoping for engagement and "likes." Let's face it—we *sell* ourselves all the time.

Whether you are saying "*choose me,*" "*read me,*" "*look at me,*" or "*listen to me,*" you are competing to capture the attention of someone else to give you the opportunity to express yourself and say, "*I have what you need at this time.*"

Ultimately we want to share our gifts and then receive something in return. It is human nature and results in a "win/win." It all begins with selling yourself.

As an expert sales trainer and coach, I get frustrated watching talented people like Dave enter the sales industry with high hopes and then leave within a year (or less), waving the white flag of failure.

Depending on which research you embrace, the occurrence of failure in the sales industry within the first four years is anywhere from 75 to 90%. That is a huge number of people failing. Why?

---

8   George W. Dudley and Shannon L. Goodson, *The Psychology of Sales-Call Reluctance: Earning What You're Worth* (Dallas: Behavioral Sciences Research Press, 2007).

There are many reasons, but if we look again to the 80/20 rule, I believe that most fail because they do not master what I call the *Seven Core Pillars of Sales Success*. These are the building blocks of a successful sales career, and they also apply to self-promotion in every area of life. In fact, they are the foundations of success in both business and life.

Pillar 1: Be the Best YOU and Live in Authenticity

Embracing who you are and the many gifts you bring to the world is at the core of all success, including sales success. My co-author Steven Sanchez says,

"People buy from people they know, like, and trust. This is why it is so important in any sales negotiation that the person buys YOU first. When you are authentic, you are actually building the trust they need so they can safely arrive at the right buying decision for their situation."[9]

Steven is so right. People want to know that the person across the table is who they are presenting themselves to be—the real deal—for better or worse. Trust is built when you know authenticity and integrity are present.

The secret is to present the best version of YOU to the world while living in authenticity. Appropriate dress for the circumstances, good grooming, good etiquette, respecting societal norms, etc. give you the outer credibility that lets you reveal your inner self. The better you present yourself while maintaining your uniqueness and authenticity, the more doors of opportunity will open.

Pillar 2: Integrity——Align with Your Passions

Doing what you say you are going to do is a BIG DEAL in developing trust. So is doing what is right. Sales success and success in general are dependent on always doing the right thing (even when it is costly and potentially painful!).

A wise mentor of mine defined integrity quite simply as *"what you do when nobody is looking."* Do you take shortcuts? Do you do

---

9   See Steven Sanchez's chapter 5.

things you know are wrong? If you do, even when people are looking, you are wearing a sign that says *I AM OUT OF INTEGRITY.*

I don't know the biomechanics of it, but trust me, people know! When that sign is hanging around your neck, it is hard to develop trust, and without trust, there is no interest in what you have to offer.

Another component of integrity is aligning yourself with your passions. If you are not passionate about something, all the acting classes in the world are not going to convince someone you are. Belief in what you are selling or promoting to the world is a critical ingredient and can't be faked. If you are not passionate about it, you have two choices:

- Improve the product and make it something you can believe in.
- Find another product to sell or promote. (If the product is *you*, then number two is not an option, so focus on number one.)

Pillar 3: Clarity of Your Goals

Find EXACTLY what you want and why you want it. Goal setting is *not* just writing a bunch of numbers or goals on a piece of paper and sliding it into a drawer next to your holiday card list for reference next year.

Know what you want and the reasons behind it. What does it mean to your life and your legacy? How does it tie to your values? How does it connect to what is most meaningful inside you?

Men and women by nature are willing to die for the things that are *most* important to them. Are your goals that meaningful to you? Do they have enough pull to get you through a day? A week? A year? Three years? Five years? They should be. If they are not, then they are not strong enough, clear enough, or tied to the things that are most meaningful to you—in which case you probably need to revisit them. Goals, and your progress toward them, must be visited with regularity (at least monthly).

Pillar 4: Calendar Discipline

We all have the same 1,440 minutes in every day. Why do some people succeed at a high level and others do not? Much of that answer lies in how we invest those 1,440 units of time each day. How well do you leverage them? How well you use your minutes and hours each day are in direct proportion to your income and your success.[10]

Pillar 5: Persistence and Energy

The definition of "persist" is *"to continue steadfastly or firmly in some state, purpose, course of action, or the like, especially in spite of opposition, etc."* Simply put, it means that you are the Energizer Bunny—you keep beating the drum and pushing forward, no matter what. Regardless of rejection, closed doors, unanswered messages, etc., you just keep kissing frogs until you find your prince!

Did you know that 80% of sales are made somewhere between the fifth and the 12th contact? And only 8% of salespeople make more than five contacts? You can do the math, and that should help explain the value of persistence. By the way, this is true in life too!

Persistence requires energy. Pick three small changes you can make in your diet and/or lifestyle for the next 30 days. Monitor your progress and track your increase in energy.[11] Your ability to be persistent will grow proportionately as well.

Pillar 6: Surround Yourself with Greatness

Who do you surround yourself with? Choose these people carefully because they will determine your success. Do they give you energy or do they suck it out of you like a Shop-Vac? Do they make you think bigger or smaller? Do they support your goals or make fun of them?

Who you surround yourself with is who you will ultimately become. That is a big statement, so take it in and think about it. They say you can choose your friends but you can't choose your family. With that said, go find at least one mentor—someone who has the

---

10   See Rita Ferguson's chapter 6.
11   See Barbara Anne Cookson's chapter 7.

success you want in an area of your life that matters most—and then find a way to spend time around that person, even if it is just buying them coffee once a month to start.

Ultimately, I recommend finding five influential people who can be your official (or even unofficial) mentors. Pick mentors in areas that are important to you. Some suggested areas for mentoring include:

- Life
- Relationships
- Business
- Financial
- Sales
- Fitness/health/energy
- Spiritual
- Contribution and giving back

Once you find them, find a way to spend as much time around them as possible.

Pillar 7: Get Creative and Differentiate!

We live in a noisy world where everyone is selling and promoting. Living the Seven Core Pillars will definitely make you stand out as the best of the best. However, on the front end—in order to get doors to open—you have to employ your creativity. The world we live in today is feverishly trying to get our attention, and sales and marketing tend to follow patterns.

Right now, sales and marketing lean more toward an impersonal approach (digital advertising, social media, text messaging, etc.). In order to open doors, while everyone else is *zigging* you need to *zag*, and that means getting personal (phone calls, handwritten notecards, and personal visits).

The point is that when everyone else is doing *this* (whatever *this* is), you need to be doing *this*, but you also need to be doing *that*.

Embrace your creativity and dare to be a little different! Creativity plus persistence is a guarantee for opening doors!

Now comes the moment of truth for you.

Like our friend Dave, we all have choices:

Do you say, "*interesting*," and move on with reading (and your life)?

Or do you pause and make a *written* commitment to take action on any of the Seven Core Pillars that could have a profound impact on your success?

The choice is yours. My hope is that you join me on the journey to a better business and life.

PAT SKIFFINGTON is an entrepreneur, author, coach, speaker, consultant and internationally-recognized business expert. Founder of the Seven Pillars of Sales Success, Pat is a sales leader and trainer with a well-defined system and passion for helping organizations and individuals reach their full potential. Learn more about Pat in "Meet The Experts."

4

I HATE MY SILVER MEDAL!

Helena Nyman

The silence in the room immediately turned into an agitated conversation among the group of top executives. The CEO of the company had called an emergency meeting due to the financial crisis of the company, and I was invited as the troubleshooter.

Despite the great talent pool among their employees, the company was failing miserably.

As a former coach for Olympic athletes I knew that the only way to break through that wall was to take the direct approach without sugarcoating the situation. I had done the diagnostic of the business situation, the culture, and the leadership, and I came to the conclusion that we were dealing with a talented team that could have gone for the gold. Instead, they had performed at the silver level.

There was no clarity about the end goal, no alignment across the organization, no laser focus, no communication, no engagement, and most importantly no fire within.

In sports, the difference between the silver medal and the gold medal performance can be represented by the following: In the example of the 2013 U.S. Open golf tournament, the winner, Justin Rose, won $1,440,000; Jason Day and Phil Mickelson, who tied for second, each won $696,104. This is a difference of $743,896.

Nobody remembers the silver medal winner's name. They are referred to as the "first loser." In business, coming in second can mean that you have to close your doors.

Steven Sanchez remembers: *"At the Beijing Olympics of 2008, swimmer Michael Phelps barely beat out Milorad Čavić by 1/100th of a second in the 100-meter butterfly. Čavić had beaten Phelps during the preliminary heats, had the fastest time in the semi-finals and was clearly ahead of Phelps even at the end. However, at the finish, Čavić coasted in but Phelps gave it one more half-stroke and won the gold by a fraction of a second. Whenever I feel like 'coasting,' I remind myself of this race and that the difference between gold and silver might be whether I make that little extra effort. The 'right' choice, when things really matter, is to leave nothing back and always give it everything you have. You never know when that little extra makes all the difference."*[12]

This is actually the norm. Most people have what it takes to perform at the gold level yet end up with a silver medal. In fact, only 1% of individuals perform at the gold level, and more than 90% of organizations cannot successfully execute their strategies.

Perhaps you've known someone like this: Everything they touch turns into gold, yet they don't come close to your experience or your talents. They work far less than you, but they still end up on the winner's podium. Gets to you, doesn't it?

Take Sally, for example. Two years ago, Sally started her own fashion design studio. Today, she wines and dines with the most

---

12 See Steven Sanchez's chapter 5.

famous fashion moguls, designs the seasonal collections for high-end boutiques, and just hired her 10th employee.

John presented his prototype of an innovative patient management program to a major medical software developer and got the funding to perfect his prototype with the promise of a partnership—and he is just starting out in his field!

What about the companies that are thriving despite the global economic crisis?

Company XYZ had one of their best years. They increased their revenue by 30% and got a national reward for customer satisfaction, and when you walk into their office you are greeted by a cheerful team.

These are the gold medalists. They play to win. They are solution oriented, not problem oriented. And it works.

What is it that holds you back from performing at the gold level? What are you afraid of?

Let's go back to the crisis meeting at the beginning of this chapter, and I'll walk you through how they got from silver to gold.

After an initial push back the leaders opened their minds and became willing to shift their mindset and their behaviors and found clarity about what they wanted to achieve. They created a powerful and exciting shared vision and were now ready to turn the vision to action.

It was incredible to observe the transformation among those leaders. Once the ice was broken and they finally revealed the sparks and fire within, there was an open communication flow, creative ideas made their way to the forefront, and they finally had clarity on what their end goal was and the direction they wanted to take to get there.

Vague goals create vague outcomes; clear goals—with appropriate and laser-focused action—create a successful outcome. And they were getting closer to making it happen.

The second hurdle was to create alignment among the top leadership and to get them to understand that every single employee of their organization needed to be a part of the process. As a united force, they were able to engage their employees in their vision, and for the first time in many years the leaders met with each department and listened to their ideas. Being appreciated and heard by their leaders was a huge game changer for the employees.[13]

It was as if someone had turned on the light switch in this company. People met in their offices to continue their conversations. They stayed after hours and came in earlier to work to brainstorm on some of their ideas. They created action teams, and after a few weeks, they presented to the executive team an action plan that would not only turn the business around but also make them a serious contender as the market leader.

Today, they are number one in their market and are driving their business stronger than ever.

It takes a team to create an empire. You can't do it alone.

Many leaders are so task-oriented that they forget about their people and leave all that potential untapped. When you ask them what comes first, they answer, *"It's about the shareholders and the bottom line"* or *"the customer is first."*

That's short-sighted and starts to create a downward spiral. Here is the proven truth:

> *If you take care of your employees, they will take very good care of your customers, and when your customers are happy, they take care of the bottom line.*

This concept does not only apply in business. It works at home, in sports, in medicine, and in charity.

The happiest and healthiest families have outstanding communication and respect among each other. They listen to each other, they are aligned, they co-create the family life, and they understand that they are a strong family only when they support each other. They know how to bring out the best in each other and all have the same outcome in mind: a loving and caring relationship.

---

13   The Gallup Organization ran a study that showed that employees ranked being fully appreciated and involved in the process as their top priority (1 and 2) while high wages and promotions only ranked 5 and 7.

The same principle applies in sports for winning teams: The coach and the team members are aligned with each other and know that every member is equally important in making a strong team.

A team cannot consist only of all A-level players or stars like the legendary Wayne Gretzky; they would miserably fail. It takes a coach, goalies, a great defense, centers, and wings. A good coach and good teammates know how to bring out the best out in each other. All have the same outcome in mind—victory!

As Pat Skiffington says, *"High performance is often framed as an individual benchmark when it should be thought of as a team goal and engagement, and combined focus."* [14]

In medicine, it takes a diagnostician, a surgeon, nurses, the anesthesiologist, and the supporting team to be focused on a common goal: the welfare of the patient.

When people volunteer for charities, they make great things happen only when they are all focused on the greater good and on making a difference.

Top performers have these six traits in common:

1. They have clarity about what they want to achieve.
2. They can see, smell, and feel the successful outcome.
3. They have a burning fire inside, a desire that gives them the strength and power of a locomotive.
4. They are unstoppable.
5. They have the ambition and willpower to turn every obstacle into a stepping-stone.
6. **They take action!**

You can have the most powerful vision and goal and the best plan, but if you don't take action, it will always stay a vision.

If I were sitting next to you and I asked you to share with me what you truly want, would you be able to do so? I dare you to be honest with yourself. Are you giving up on your dream because

---

14 See Pat Skiffington's chapter 3.

you don't want to appear pompous? Did you learn that modesty is a virtue? Don't confuse being confident with being arrogant.

In all areas of life, including sports and business, people suffer from the same basic unhappiness. They feel they have never been able to go for the gold in their area.

I dare you to be unique, grandiose, a genius! It's your life.[15] You are responsible for your actions and your results.

The following three action steps will send you on an incredible journey to experience how it feels to touch the gold. If you are already putting your efforts into what you are doing, why not go the whole way for the gold? It feels pretty darn good.

3 Steps to Your Gold Medal

Action Step 1

Find a place that inspires you! A mountain peak, the ocean beach, a deep forest, whatever it is for you. Close your eyes and dare to dream. What is it really that you want? Not *"I would like . . . "*

Be very specific! Dream big! Test the result by asking yourself if your dream would really qualify for the gold medal. Imagine yourself reaping the fruits of your success. Can you see it? Can you smell it? Can you feel the goose bumps?

Action Step 2

Can you identify anyone who has reached the gold medal level that you want, or are you a pioneer? In either case, how is that gold medal situation different from the situation you are currently in? What are three things you could do immediately to move closer to reaching your dream? Interview other gold medal performers to ask them how they got there!

---

15   If you're the spouse or partner of someone who keeps you stifled in the spotlight, I encourage you to read Joyce Sawyer's tips in chapter 9 and get advice on thriving in that role.

Action Step 3

Take action! Get out of your paralysis and take a leap of faith. Map out your next steps with measurable goals and a timeline. If necessary, surround yourself with supporters and have an accountability buddy. Adjust your course if necessary.

Consistency and persistence are the keys to your gold. If you have truly found your ultimate dream and goal, be inspired and use your fuel to overcome any obstacle that stands in your way.

Perform at the Gold Medal Level and win! You can do it!

HELENA NYMAN is an expert on high performance with a passion for helping people unlock their full potential and reach their peak performance. Learn more about Helena in "Meet the Experts."

5

HOW DO YOU KNOW WHEN SOMETHING'S "RIGHT" FOR YOU?

Steven Sanchez

P*lease help me! EXACTLY how should I set up my website?"* Terri's plea seemed urgent, almost desperate. And she wasn't the only one.

We were attending a social media workshop. The speaker had done a good job presenting the importance of blogging, having a Facebook page, creating a YouTube video channel, etc., but completely missed her audience. While the information was accurate, it was overwhelming. People were presented many choices but didn't know how to choose the *right* ones for their particular situation.

Rose Sheehan says, *"Creating and engaging in the use of a powerful social media platform is paramount to any business that wants to thrive*

30

in this fiercely competitive global economy."[16] But still—how do you know which choice is right?

After the event, the audience was full of questions. *"Should I set up a website or a blog first?" "Do I use WordPress or Blogger?" "How do I link Facebook to my website?"* The questions came fast and furious. People were desperate to know the right answers for their particular situation. Understandably so. There are thousands of decisions to make and making the right choices for your particular situation can be overwhelming. Add in marketing and social media and it's enough to make you cry.

We've all felt the frustration of needing to make the "right" choice in an important situation. Should I stay at my job or look for something else? Where should we go for a vacation this year? Is this the right investment for my family's future? Make a mistake and you've lost not only time and money, you may have even changed the course of your life.

How Do You Make The "Right" Choice?

Wouldn't it be nice if there were a way of *guaranteeing* you made the *right* choice? You know, like putting all the variables into a computer and out spits, say, the exact location of Willy Wonka's golden ticket. What would life look like if you could consistently make the right choices? What could you accomplish if you had a *method* for making the best decision, particularly for you, every time? How much further could you get in your job or your life if you knew the right steps to take?

Could there be a *scientific* way of making right choices? After all, every day you make thousands of decisions that get you through the day safely and successfully, from what to wear in the morning to which shortcut you'll take coming home.

You already make thousands of decisions every day. So there must be some method that you're using, maybe on a subconscious level, to

---

16   See Rose Sheehan's chapter 16.

help you make good choices and correct for unexpected problems. But what about new things you've never seen before?

The number of people figuring out how to make right choices with new challenges is absolutely staggering:

- More new Facebook profiles are created every second than there are people being born.
- Google+ adds approximately 625,000 new users daily.
- Every day 350 million photos are uploaded to Facebook, about 4,000 photos per second.
- Approximately 100 hours of video are uploaded to YouTube every minute.
- Every minute of the day approximately 571 new websites are created.
- 55% of Americans ages 45–54 have a profile on a social networking site, and they are the fastest growing demographic.

Imagine what *you* could accomplish if you could rely upon a decision-making *method* and employ it whenever you're facing a new challenge.

Presenting the Results-Research-Rewards System™

There *is* a way you can scientifically work your way to the best decision for you, every time. I call it the Results-Research-Rewards System™. It's similar to the process improvement system Rita Ferguson, an expert in project management, collaborative author, and friend, speaks about. She says,

"One of the basic principles of process improvement is the Think-Plan-Do cycle. I use variations of this handy rule in so many ways, including making important choices. When it comes to choices, including purchasing software, I change it to Think-Plan-Choose!"[17]

Whenever you need to figure out the right choice for you or your business, here are the steps I recommend you take.

---

17   See Rita Ferguson's chapter 6.

Step 1: List the RESULTS You Want from the Choice That Are IMPORTANT to You

Everything starts with your purpose. This is where you decide *why* the decision is important to you. Co-author Pat Skiffington puts it this way:

"*Making decisions with your purpose in mind is the only way to set yourself up for success. Emotional decision making decreases your odds. Always use an objective, logical method of narrowing your field of choices to the one choice that makes the most sense for your desired outcome, which will put you on course to achieve your purpose.*"[18]

Begin by listing what it is you are trying to achieve:

- What <u>results</u> will making the right choice allow you to *have*?
- What will making the right choice gain you that you don't have now?
- What <u>new capabilities</u> will this choice enable you to *do*?
- Will this choice allow you to do things you couldn't do before? Will this choice give you new opportunities or open new doors?
- What <u>difference</u> will making the right choice help you to *be*?
- What personal status will making the right choice gain you? Will you have a new title others will recognize and value? Is this something on your "bucket list"?

My friend and fellow author Barry Laub also encourages professionals to get in touch with their why. His Purpose-Objective-Plan formula is in complete alignment with this approach. He believes that this is the key in business and life to achieve your why.[19]

When you start with why, you identify what's most important to YOU about this choice. It also helps you filter out things that might be interesting but that actually distract from your getting to what you truly want. So start by making a checklist of the things you really want.

---

18 See Pat Skiffington's chapter 3.
19 See Barry Laub's chapter 13.

Step 2: Identify Three to Five CHOICES or Solutions That You Think Might Be a Fit for Your List

Now it's time to pick a few choices you could make that could pass most or all of the checklist you just created. When you choose a restaurant, you don't open the phone book and go down the list. You come up with a short list based on advertising, word-of-mouth, and personal experience.

In this step you'll come up with your own short list of choices that fit your checklist above.

- Which choices have caught your attention?
- Which might make the cut because you have visited their website, have seen their commercial, or had your curiosity piqued and you're still interested?
- Which choices are friends or family most familiar with?
- Now it's time to bring in your social filter. What do the people you know and trust think about a choice?
- Which choices do review sites consider to be the best?

Time to bring in the wisdom of experts. Today, there's almost always a website that reviews and rates the best available choices.

So, you've got a checklist of everything that's important to you about this decision, and you've come up with three to five possible choices that meet your criteria and that you're still interested in, people you trust like, and experts endorse. Now it's time to pick the "right" one for you.

Step 3: Choose the Solution That Rewards You Best with Everything You Want to Be, Do, and Have for the Immediate Future

Okay, truth be told, probably ANY of the three to five choices that made the first two cuts would be just fine. But we're on the hunt for the "right" choice for you. Here's where the magic really happens.

You've got a checklist and a list. Now it's time to make a grid, or use a spreadsheet if it's handy. Down one side list the three to five choices you are still considering. Across the top, make three columns labeled BE, DO, HAVE, and TOTAL. Your Be-Do-Have weighting grid should look like this:

What I Want to Be, Do, and Have			
	Be	**Do**	**Have**	**Total**
Choice 1				
Choice 2				
Choice 3				
Choice 4				
Choice 5				

Now for each choice, give each one a number from 1 to 5 (depending upon how many choices you have) in each column.

1 = FEELS wrong, DOES nothing, HAS *no* value

2 = FEELS like something's not right, DOES little, HAS *low* value

3 = FEELS neither right or wrong, DOES help me achieve but not excel, HAS *reasonable* value

4 = FEELS good, DOES get me closer to my goals, HAS *good* value

5 = FEELS perfect, DOES give me the best chance for results, HAS the *best* value

When you're all done your completed grid should look something like this.

What I Want to Be, Do, and Have			
	Be	Do	Have	Total
Choice 1	4	3	5	12
Choice 2	5	5	4	14
Choice 3	3	4	3	10
Choice 4	2	2	1	5
Choice 5	1	1	2	4

Not only can you see which choice has the greatest overall total (as does choice 2 above), you can also sort on the columns to rank your choices for each column.

So what has using the Results-Research-Rewards System™ given you?

- You've listed what's most important to you in a checklist that is useful for screening possible choices.
- You've identified three to five choices that passed your initial test and are worthy of more careful consideration.
- You've ranked your short list based on quality, performance, and ROI.

You can now look at your choices and identify which choice you've *scientifically* evaluated to be the right choice for you.

Doing It Quickly

The amazing thing is that our brains compress this process into a split-second decision every time we drive a car. We decide what we want to do, consider our possible choices based on past experience, determine what we think we should do, and decide based on the best decision that will get us what we want to be, do, and have; where we want to go; how quickly we want to get there; and how safely we want to arrive.

Today, my formerly overwhelmed friend Terri has a beautiful website that she set up herself. Whenever she hits a bump and needs help making a choice, I'll usually get a call. However, when she can't reach me, all she has to do is jot down what's important to her, do a little Google research on the most recommended choices for her particular problem, and then rank them by what she wants to be, do, and have in the shortest time possible. Now you can do that too.

The next time you have to make a decision and find yourself stopped at the fork in the road, go through this Results-Research-Rewards System™.

See if it doesn't help you get to what you want to be, do, and have. As my friend and co-author Wendy Lipton-Dibner always says, *"Life is far too short to settle for less than you truly want—in your business or your life."*

STEVEN SANCHEZ has been building custom websites for more than 20 years. Over that time he has helped everyone from children's workers to cruise liners develop and implement the right solutions for their unique and particular business objectives. Learn more about Steven in "Meet the Experts."

6

TOO BUSY TO MAKE MORE MONEY?

Rita Ferguson

"Business is good and we are busy!"

Greg is the owner of a small, profitable business that designs specialty restaurant equipment. We met at an industry meeting in Chicago and became engaged in a discussion about the joys and pain points of small business ownership.

"The downside is I'm so busy with the day-to-day activities that I can't find the time to start on some new concepts I've got knocking around in my head!" Greg sighed.

Greg's problem is typical for small business owners. I'd seen that growing up. I was raised in a family of entrepreneurs and worked for the family business through high school and college. After completing my degree, I chose a path working for several Fortune

500 companies and came to finally appreciate the herculean efforts of small business owners.

In a large corporation, I had access to a wide range of resources at my fingertips. If I needed a legal opinion, I called the legal department. Launch a new product? Call corporate marketing. Personnel issues? Call human resources! Insurance, 401(k) plans, tax issues, financial planning, you name it—all were handled within the big corporate structure called "headquarters."

Not so for entrepreneurs, who are ultimately responsible for all of it. No wonder small business owners are too busy to make more money!

Greg continued, *"How in the world do I implement new ideas when I'm caught in the daily whirlwind of activity?"*

I replied, *"Handle those new ideas as projects. Put project management structure to them."*

He took a deep breath. *"I've got a small business. I don't want anything too complicated!"*

I was a project manager in the corporate world, and that skill set is what made my own small business successful. Project management is not just for elaborate projects like building a tunnel under a seaway. It is the best strategy for small business and small teams.

I asked Greg about that new product floating around in his head, *"What's your strategic plan? Where do you see your business in three years? Does your new concept support the strategy?"*

"My strategic plan is to make more money!" he smiled.

"Sure, making money is every businessman's goal, but HOW are you going to do that?"

"Well, I know what I want to do, but I don't have a written plan," he replied.

81% of small business owners are not strategic.

Greg is not alone in underestimating the importance of defining and assessing a plan.

In a 2014 national survey of small business owners, 81% of respondents said they do not consider themselves strategic when it comes to decision making.[20]

The main reason given by business owners for not thinking or planning strategically: *"Too busy."*

Think Strategically

Thinking strategically means: **decisions we make today must take into consideration future trends and economic factors.**

When we think strategically, our business strategies are based on our current knowledge of our industry (real facts) and a gut feeling based on what we expect will happen in the future.

Seven Steps to Create Your Strategic Small Business Plan

Step 1: Know your industry. Attend industry seminars. Read trade magazines and online newsletters. What do you see happening? How can you be a leader in your industry?

Step 2: Know your competitors. Track what they are doing. Check out their websites. Network with them at industry meetings.

Step 3: Know your customers. What are their future needs? What do they see happening in THEIR industries? If you don't know, ask them. You may find a valuable joint venture partner.

Step 4: Connect all your employees to your vision. What do THEY see happening in the next three to five years in the industry, with your competitors, with your customers?

Step 5: Create a self-development plan for yourself and your employees to maintain a high level of excellence and performance. What future skills, special knowledge, or coaching do you and your employees need in order to position yourself for changes in your industry?

---

20 Bank of America, "Small Business Report," Spring 2014.

Step 6: Know your community. In which ways can your small business be of service? What are other ways you can give back?

Step 7: Plan your products. Strategic thinking could also produce a wake-up call that your product or service may be obsolete in a few years. What new product or new service can you provide? Can you take your business in a completely different direction?

> *The plan still in your head is no plan at all—*
> *it's only an idea that can shift, change, or be forgotten!*

Even if your future vision is only a few sentences in each area, write it out. Once in written form, you can tweak it and fill in the details as they become more clear to you. Put it where you can see it every day. Keep it in front of your eyes and in the forefront of your mind.

Several weeks after the conference, my new friend Greg surprised me with a phone call. *"How can I prototype and launch quickly?,"* he asked.

He was so excited after our conversation that he went straight home and called a strategic thinking session with his management team. They went through the seven steps I've outlined for you above, and Greg finally saw that his new product—the one still in sketch phase—could be extremely lucrative. His new product was the grand-slam home run that business owners dream about!

Pick Your Project!

Your strategic plan will determine which opportunities you go after now, the ones you go after later, and the ones you will not pursue at all.

When you decide on a new opportunity, make sure you ask five questions:

1. Why am I selecting THIS project?
2. How does it relate to the business plan?

3. What is the benefit it brings?
4. What would happen if I did not select this project?
5. What would be the effect on my business by not doing it? (Be your own devil's advocate!)

5 Project Management Steps to Get You Started

Step 1: Determine the Deliverable of the Project

Project planning starts with a clearly documented description or sketch or picture of the intended end product, or "deliverable." The deliverable is the product, service, or outcome you'll have when the project is complete.

The project plan bridges the gap from today to the completion of the project. It is critical that the deliverable be well defined so you will know when the project is complete.

Step 2: Create a Task List

Now that you have a clear description of the deliverable, get your team together and brainstorm what needs to be done to make it happen. Look for all the "ugly" tasks and get them listed as well.

- Who is going to do what and how long will it take?
- What need to be done first?
- Which tasks cannot be started until another task has finished?
- Which tasks can be done at the same time?
- What about downstream effects of the project? Look for changes that may need to be made to your current procedures either during or after the project.

Step 3: Create the Plan

The project plan breaks down the work into doable steps that ultimately create the deliverable. It includes the resources required (time, people, supplies, etc.) and the target dates.

Consider the challenges that may arise and the risks associated with the challenges. Is your project schedule realistic? Is your budget realistic? What would happen if there was a delay or cost overrun? How would you handle it? Write down the risk and write out the response. If that risk should occur, you will be prepared to handle it.

Step 4: Implement (Do It and Stick to It!)

It's time to work the plan! Rose Sheehan, an entrepreneur and author, says, *"We all have the same number of hours in a day. The secret is to consciously decide how we want to spend the time we have on our goals. It is critical to prioritize, plan, delegate, and do. Without the first three, the 'do' is fruitless."*[21]

You spent a lot of time laying a firm foundation with thinking and planning. But results come from doing! As my colleague Steve Sanchez correctly points out,

"Right Idea + Right Execution = Success!"[22]

Your job is to clear the path for your team so they can implement the plan. If you will be actively involved, seize control of your agenda to avoid distractions.

Pat Skiffington says, *"For most business owners, assuming you have mastered your strategic plan and built a team of talented people, the answer is truly effective time management and project management systems. Master these and the sky is the limit!"*[23]

Create blocks of time within the day for project work. Stay focused and on track. Work the plan, but be flexible if the unexpected arises or if business conditions change. Tweak the plan if needed, but persevere!

---

21 See Rose Sheehan's chapter 16.
22 See Steve Sanchez's chapter 5.
23 See Pat Skiffington's chapter 3.

Step 5: Celebrate!

When the project is successful, celebrate with your team! Enjoy your accomplishment and be assured that the next project is lurking around the corner!

Since you are reading these words in a book classified as success literature, I know you are a person who has heightened ambitions for your life. Do more than just read this chapter—put it into daily PRACTICE!

As a business owner, you are already on a great journey. Whether you have been on your entrepreneurial trek for many years or are just getting started, you will be delighted with your results when your daily agenda is in sync with your long-term goals. Your business will then be positioned to meet future challenges, and, best of all, you will feel energized and productive.

These simple techniques work, regardless of the size of your business or the type of product or service you offer. Create a written plan for your business to turn your ideas into reality!

RITA FERGUSON challenges small business owners and corporate managers to think strategically and to use project management techniques to align their daily activities with their short- and long-term goals. She is a small business owner with a solid background in project management and operational process improvement. Learn more about Rita in "Meet the Experts."

7

THE CIRCLE OF HAPPY AND HEALTHY

Barbara Anne Cookson, LMT, CHC

When I first met Janet she was 52 years old and felt lost. "I work in a doctor's office, and I see people every day who are my age and struggling with their health. It's my job to get all their information when they come in. They're so overweight and on so many medications! I don't want to end up like them!"

Janet went on to tell me she was tired all the time and never felt strong. Her son was going to be married, and all she wanted was to fit into that beautiful purple dress for the wedding and feel good about herself. She imagined her future with grandchildren and shared how much she wanted to be healthy and strong enough to play with them and *"do what I want to do."*

I wish I could tell you Janet's concerns are unique, but the truth is that I hear this every day. According to research by the Centers for Disease Control and the National Center for Health Statistics in 2012, 69% of adults age 20 and over are overweight or obese.[24]

Depression (unhappiness) affects one in 10 Americans at one point or another, and the number of patients diagnosed with depression increases by approximately 20% per year. *"Personal happiness is generally considered to be the ultimate goal in life."*[25]

Life is a circle of happy and healthy, unhappy and unwell. We all want to be on the happy, healthy side of the circle, but happiness is different for everyone. For example, playing golf does **not** make me happy. Knocking around a little ball for hours is my idea of hell. But I have friends who absolutely love to golf! It makes them HAPPY!

What if we could choose our own happiness and bring it to life? What if we could live on the bright side of the circle?

My mom asked me recently, *"What makes you happy?"*

I answered, *"Everything!"*

But it wasn't always that way.

From the time I was 19, I worked as a dental assistant. Yet when I turned 40, I found myself wondering if that was what I really wanted. At the time I was 30 pounds overweight and totally sedentary. My family was in crisis mode, taking care of my dad, who had endured a kidney transplant, heart bypass and valve replacement, gall bladder surgery, double hip replacement, vascular disease resulting in the loss of both legs above the knee, and the removal of numerous skin cancers.[26]

Everyone who knew my dad said he was the most upbeat, positive person they'd ever met. Despite his declining health, he kept a happy outlook. He *chose* to be happy. Do you?

---

24 "Health, United States, 2013: With Special Feature on Prescription Drugs" (Hyattsville, MD: National Center for Health Statistics, 2014), table 64, http://www.cdc.gov/data/hus/hus13.pdf.

25 Michael W. Fordyce, *Human Happiness: Its Nature and Its Attainment* (2000).

26 If you or a loved one is dealing with a health crisis of your own, please read my friend Lesley Graham's chapter 14.

According to the Mayo Clinic, *"studies show that personality traits like optimism and pessimism can affect many areas of your health and well-being."* 27

Over the years, I've studied and read everything I can get my hands on about mind-body wellness. I needed to find the secrets to get to and stay in the happy and healthy side of the circle.

I got a trainer. I got healthy. I became a fitness instructor. I went back to school and became a licensed massage therapist and later a Certified Holistic Health Coach. And throughout that process, I discovered there are common turns on the circle that successful people need to make in order to reach their goals.

The 5 Turns to Happy and Healthy

Turn 1

Highlight the things you are grateful for in your life. The first assignment I give all my coaching clients is to start a gratitude journal. A study conducted in 2003 found, *"Those who kept a gratitude journal on a weekly basis exercised more regularly, reported fewer physical symptoms, and felt better about their lives as a whole."* 28 The study also found,

"Participants who kept gratitude lists were more likely to have made progress toward important personal goals."

DO THIS: Get a small notebook or journal and pen to keep on your nightstand. Take a few moments at bedtime to jot down three to five things you are thankful for today. Remembering the positives from your day may just help you sleep better!

---

27   Mayo Clinic Staff, "Positive Thinking: Stop Negative Self-Talk to Reduce Stress," Mayo Clinic website, March 4, 2014, http://www.mayoclinic.org/art20043950.

28   R. A. Emmons and M. E. McCullough, eds., *The Psychology of Gratitude* (New York: Oxford University Press, 2003).

Turn 2

Acknowledge that you are not perfect. It's totally okay to make mistakes. It's even okay if your thighs rub together. We put so much pressure on ourselves to have the perfect body, to have the picture-perfect home, to be the perfect mom, dad, spouse, whatever. Enough already! Allow yourself to be perfectly, uniquely, imperfect. Truly loving our own imperfections has healing power. Loving ourselves not only creates happiness but also contributes to our overall health.

> **DO THIS:** Identify the "imperfections" in your loved ones. Make a list. (Don't make this into a gripe session; it's all about seeing that "imperfections" are okay.) Under that list, write down all the reasons you love them. Understanding that you can love others with all of their "imperfections" will allow you to love yourself no matter what you see in the mirror.

Turn 3

Post your "wants and wishes" where you can see them every day. My friend Barry Laub, master of mindset and attitude, says, *"You can alter your mindset by deciding and choosing."* [29] Choose your wants and wishes from your heart with passion and with intent to be happy.

> **DO THIS:** Create a Circle of Happy and Healthy board. You can use a bulletin board, poster board, or even a notebook. If you're a computer whiz, there are software programs or apps available, too. [30] On it, post pictures, thoughts, words, and other things that truly create a visual of your happy, healthy life.

Turn 4

Pretend! Do you remember when you were a kid and tied a towel around your neck to wear like a cape? You pretended with all your

---

29 See Barry Laub's chapter 13.
30 For Mac, try Success Vision Board and Dream Vision Board. For Windows, there's Vision Board Builder.

heart to be a superhero. You **felt** like a superhero! You acted like you could fly! That's the kind of pretending I mean. This is key: You have to feel like you've already achieved your vision of your happy and healthy self.

Project yourself into the future and **feel, act, think, be, and do like you're already there.** You're living the dream, baby! Close your eyes and feel the emotions, the joy, the satisfaction from living the happy, healthy life you've created for yourself.

> **DO THIS:** Practice pretending. Spend focused, concentrated time on this one. Start out with 15 minutes in the morning with your Circle of Happy and Healthy board. Close your eyes and imagine yourself doing, having, or being what you've posted there. Once you can picture it vividly in your mind—the sights, smells, and sounds—now **feel** the emotions that go along with your vision. Here's an example: Say your vision is of a healthy, slim, fit you. Close your eyes and picture yourself in the dress. Remember the color? What does the fabric feel like? See the whole you, new shoes, jewelry, and that dream date. Now feel it. Feel the emotions, the excitement, the power in your strong body and the satisfaction of knowing you look awesome!

Turn 5

Say **Y**es!!!!! As adults, we are notorious for "should-ing" ourselves right out of any fun. Remember Janet? One of her wants was to have more creative time in her schedule. When I asked what was keeping her from just doing it, she replied, "*Well, there's the housework, and the meals, and time for my husband*[31] *and taking care of my mom . . .*" There were dozens of things on her list, proof that she wasn't allowing herself play time. The belief that we need to be productive every

---

31   For more on healthy, happy relationships, see Joyce Sawyer's chapter 9.

minute needs to stop. Give yourself permission to have, be, or do whatever your heart desires.

DO THIS: Make a permission contract with yourself. I have my clients sign a contract with themselves making the commitment to be open to new ideas, to be coachable, etc. It doesn't have to be fancy legal jargon; just list the items from your Circle of Happy and Healthy board and give yourself permission to be, have, or do all of them. In your list, remember to allow yourself time to pause and play. Here's a sample permission contract:

Date _____

I am committed to my own personal health and happiness. With this commitment, I give myself permission to:

1. _____
2. _____
3. _____
4. _____
5. _____

Signed _____

Witness[32] _____

The 5 Turns to Happy and Healthy are your beginning to living in the bright side of the circle, where you'll grow your vitality and your joy. Your happiness and health will increase with the first turn, and each turn that follows will take you even deeper into the happy and healthy circle of life.

People say that *life is not about the destination; it's about the journey.* What they don't tell you is that the journey is a circle, and when you know how to navigate that circle everything changes for you.

---

32   For many of us, it's more meaningful to make a commitment to others than to ourselves. Adding a witness to your contract gives you an accountability partner.

The bright side of your circle is just a few turns away. Take the first turn and then go through all five turns. You'll quickly become who you choose to be. How do I know?

It's been six months since Janet and I first met. If you could see the changes, you'd know exactly how powerful the 5 Turns of Happy and Healthy can be. Janet's skin is glowing and she's absolutely radiant! She's smiling from ear to ear as she hands me a beautiful spring arrangement. She's positively giddy. Without saying a word, she pulls out her phone and shows me a beautiful wedding photo with her shining in the dress she dreamed of wearing. She is happier, healthier (and smaller!) than she's been in a long time. She's exercising every day, enjoying time with her husband, and she's stronger than ever.

My question for you is: When will you take your turn in the Circle of Happy and Healthy?

BARBARA ANNE COOKSON, LMT, CHC, is a health and life coach, licensed massage therapist, and motivational speaker. She is the founder of the circleofhappyandhealthy.com, an online community dedicated to helping people live happier and healthier lives at work and at home. Learn more about Barbara in "Meet the Experts."

8

THE FORMATIVE EVENT

Marilyn Ida Horowitz

Much has been said about using writing to improve one's life, and I heartily agree with most of it. However, the advice is often too general, and the goal, which is often peace of mind, is rarely attained. While working writers want to tell stories or report on current events, the goal for the nonwriter is different. For the nonwriter, writing is a tool for almost instant clarity on many critical aspects of everyday life, a way to solve an immediate problem, to get in touch with and resolve a painful emotion, or to understand one's self on a deeper, more spiritual level.

I have been a writer, writing teacher, writing coach, and filmmaker for the last 18 years. I have a trademarked system of writing that allows writers to tell compelling stories with ease. In my work as a coach, I have helped many kinds of writers solve not just their story problems but their life problems as well. I am going to share a powerful technique that can be used to help solve challenges in your own life. It's an exercise that will get you in touch with a crucial, formative experience, and, in doing so, help you to deal with the repercussions that experience has had since.[33]

When I was six, long before I could write, I made a series of drawings of the characters in a play I'd come up with about a princess who has been locked away by her evil stepmother for a crime the princess did not commit. I made 20 drawings of the characters and the sets for the play, each of which my mother lovingly hole-punched and bound together with shiny brass fasteners. I had now written my first "book," which I proudly took to school for show-and-tell. My homeroom teacher, Mrs. Rank, whom I will never forget—a pretty, tall, blonde lady with deep green eyes—flipped through the drawings, clapped her hands with delight, and said, *"Marilyn, this is wonderful! We are going to mount this as our first grade play and perform it in front of the whole school."*

I was pleased and excited until Mrs. Rank asked, *"So, what's the story about?"* My world turned to ashes. My mother hadn't warned me that I would need a narrative to go along with the pictures! Luckily, I knew the opening line was always *"Once upon a time,"* and somehow I was able to spin a yarn on the spot. It went like this:

> Once upon a time in the land of fairy tales, it was winter and very cold where the princess was imprisoned. Her only friend was a starving raven, whom she fed from her own meager dish. A prince came along to woo the princess, but her stepmother, the evil witch, was so powerful that she had to be killed to enable the princess to escape. The prince, naturally, was good, so he was in a quandary: If he failed to kill the witch he would lose the princess. The princess, who loved her stepmother in spite of everything,

33 *"Writing slows down the mind and puts the jumble of thoughts into formation. Whether we are struggling with a personal, spiritual, business, or relational mess, writing is the first step toward a permanent solution."* See Rita Ferguson's chapter 6.

agreed that things should remain as they were and accepted her lonely fate. At that moment, the raven realized that he could help the princess who had fed him when he was hungry, and so he killed the witch himself. The three of them lived happily after.

The whole class applauded and laughed after I finished, but I was very upset because I felt I hadn't been warned about needing a story. Years later, when I was dealing with a personal issue that required therapy, the therapist looked at me and said, *"Don't you think that this experience was the formative event of your life and that all of your work as a writer, New York University professor, and writing coach has been about helping yourself and others answer this question of 'What is the story?'"* He stopped me in my tracks. I had never before connected my life's work with this early triumphant but traumatic moment.

Later on, when I sold a novel to a producer, I was asked to adapt it into a screenplay and very nearly failed. At the 11th hour I was saved by a dream in which Joseph Campbell (best known for his popular PBS television series with Bill Moyers, *The Power of Myth*) appeared before me and "dictated" a map that helped me finish the script. When I woke up and wrote down the dream, I realized that, in both writing and our daily lives, we suffer when we don't know what the story is.

My work as a coach and a writing teacher led me to take the map I received in my dream and create a trademarked writing method, The Horowitz System*, that has helped thousands of first-time writers complete an entire a screenplay in only 10 weeks.

Because my system works for all kinds of storytelling, I have also worked on screenplays, novels, nonfiction, and memoirs as a private coach. The method mirrors the way we like to hear our stories told and provides a story map to help us translate the tales hidden inside of us. Telling stories is a way to understand what our interests and concerns are, and where our values and assumptions lie. By understanding ourselves in this way, we stay connected to our dreams and goals and are more likely to make them happen.[34]

A Zen master once wrote, *"While pain is necessary, suffering is optional."* I pondered that long and hard—in terms of how it applied both to my students and to me. The answer was surprising: We suffer when we don't know what we want to do or say.[35]

Without a way to shape the stories of our lives as we currently know them, we remain victims of the assumptions and fears we hold from the past. These assumptions include cultural attitudes, self-worth assessments, whether we are worthy of self-love, and our expectations for happiness and wealth.[36]

Here's how to complete the Formative Event Exercise:

Identify the issue or problem you want to work on.[37] Then, close your eyes and try to remember something in your past that relates to the problem. There may be more than one memory, but grab whichever one comes up first—it's potential gold. For example, if you are struggling with a diet, try to recall the first time you realized that you needed to lose weight. What was the story? How did it make you feel? Were you angry? Resistant? Ashamed? And how did that experience inspire you to act? Did you go on a diet? Did you go out and binge? Did you resolve to lose weight? This memory contains the Formative Event that will become the key to greater understanding of yourself by connecting your present with your past.

Now that you have selected the problem you want to work on and recalled a related experience, set a timer for 15 minutes.

---

34 *"Whether your intent is to write an email, a memo, a journal, a report, or even a business plan; writing is a critical tool for gaining focus of mind and clarity of thought for successful communication with yourself and others in this world of information bombardment and overload."* See Rose Sheehan's chapter 16.

35 To see how not knowing what you do or say may affect your parenting and cause needless suffering, please see Ann Van De Water's chapter 10.

36 *"It is only when we bravely look behind the curtain of our childhood wounding that we can possibly grow and move beyond our unconscious knee-jerk responses."* See Lorraine Pursell's chapter 11.

37 Fiction and dramatic writers can also use the technique for developing their characters.

Write about the event. Keep in mind, this is not about writing well; it's about getting your thoughts on paper.

Reread what you wrote and apply the five W's we learned in school: who, what, where, when, and why. Then, using what you have just learned, analyze what the memory was about and how it has affected you. For example, when the therapist pointed out that I had spent my life answering the question *"What is the story?,"* it changed me forever.

Finally, based on the new connections you have just made between the past and the present, consider what, if any, changes you would want to make to the current situation you are writing about.

For example, when I first attempted the Formative Event Exercise myself, it was the story of my first play that came to mind, and so I wrote about it. When I reread the exercise the next day I was pleasantly surprised by what it revealed. The clues to why I'd spent my life trying to understand and help others write their stories suddenly made perfect sense: There had been no one there to help me when I made up the story. I realized that I must have received some kind of higher guidance to offer up a story that was so morally sophisticated.

In addition, the experience of being forced to make up a good story on the spot gave me an amazing, life-changing belief about storytelling: Somewhere, somehow, we all have a story that is ready to tell all the way through. It is complete in the imagination, not just a bunch of random thoughts.

I also felt an absolute faith that something or someone had shown up to help me—that I was not alone. As the child of atheists, I found this insight to be a big deal and decided to keep it to myself. I focused on my faith in knowing that our stories are already within us, fully formed, and that understanding our own stories would help transform nonwriters' lives. They simply needed to be made aware that we are all storytellers!

If everyone was taught to make stories out of moments in their lives as a problem-solving tool, they could easily take stock of the present, plan for the future, and solve an immediate problem. Angela Alexander says, *"The process of writing your story can be very healing and therapeutic. While writing my autobiography I saw how God built my faith, which prepared me for what could have devastated my life forever."* [38]

To summarize, the solutions I garnered from revisiting this formative event continue to inform my life choices and have become the basis for my faith in something larger than myself. Please find the time to do the Formative Event Exercise for yourself. Not only will it allow you to work concretely on a problem by looking at it from a different perspective, it may reveal for you the spiritual and/or religious beliefs that are helping or hindering you on your path to peace of mind, a worthy goal for us all.

MARILYN IDA HOROWITZ is an author, producer, writing coach, and award-winning New York University professor who has helped thousands write a screenplay in 10 weeks or less, using her trademarked writing system for screenplays and novels. She is also the author of the recent political thriller *The Book of Zev*. Learn more about Marilyn in "Meet the Experts."

---

38 See Angela Alexander's chapter 12.

›9‹

STIFLED IN THE SPOTLIGHT

Joyce Sawyer

How does it feel to be a decoration?" he asked. The question hit me hard, particularly since it came from a friend.

I'm married to a politician. That puts me in the spotlight. Or at least in the shadow of the spotlight. My husband's name is Tom Sawyer (imagine the comments I hear about that).

I expected there would be ups and downs married to a high-profile man. But it never occurred to me that I would be labeled "a decoration." That was the moment I realized I'd spent several decades living stifled in the spotlight.

Don't get me wrong. I truly love my husband—and other women who are stifled in the spotlight love their husbands as well. Around the globe, women who are married to top executives, military men, professors and ministers all love their husbands while suffering from varying degrees of Stifled Syndrome™.

Do you make your high-profile husband look good or know someone who does? If so, you are in good company.

How can a marriage survive the pressure of maintaining one's individuality, raising a healthy family, immersing oneself in a career separate from his, handling demands on your time, navigating social situations, and more?

What are the secrets to handling your public life while protecting your privacy and not losing yourself along the way?

Keeping your head above water in the fishbowl of public life isn't easy. We have so many questions about our lifestyle: *Why can't I go anywhere and just be me? Why aren't you the same at home as you are in public? Can't we ever go out without talking to everyone in the room? Do I have to go to that event? Do you realize how much your kids miss you?*

I had been teaching in the public school system for 20 years when a national publication interviewed me and asked, *"Did your husband have anything to do with you getting or keeping your job?"*

"No, but I had a hell of a lot to do with his getting and keeping his job," I replied.

My response wasn't included in the article, but I felt good about saying it, and my husband often repeats it when he refers to me as an "asset."

Being married to a power player is a challenge. Thoughts about having our own turn to shine are often mixed with feelings of being underappreciated, trapped, unhappy, resentful, alone, and "stifled." The good news is you can have a fulfilling situation as what I call a Power Spouse™.

When Linda[39] came to me, she was feeling many of the typical symptoms of being stifled in the spotlight. She viewed her marriage as *"the hardest job in American politics,"* yet didn't know how to improve it. When she gained access to the steps I'm about to give you, Linda was transformed from being a stifled, resentful spouse to one who could actually thrive. Her identity was left intact and her entire family was more content. Now when I see her out in the community, I see a

---

39 Not her real name.

woman who is truly enjoying herself, and it makes me optimistic for others. We have conversations now that convince me she is no longer stifled in the spotlight.

Linda is an example of a person who initially found her role difficult, yet today she and her husband are planning a celebration for their anniversary. She is just one of many who have discovered the secrets to Power Spousing™.

So what does it take to enjoy your role as your spouse's secret weapon? Ditch your skepticism and devote some time to following these specific steps.

18 Steps to Power Spousing™

Step 1: Find your own successes, career and otherwise, which are not a reflection of your spouse or anyone else. It's one thing to be the woman behind the powerful man; it's another to be your own powerful person and maintain your own identity.

Step 2: Pick the right partner. If he's someone you can admire and support, not only love, the Power Spouse™ role becomes far more pleasant and rewarding. His broad service to more than just himself keeps the egocentric behavior that often accompanies powerful positions at bay. Each person in a partnership should want the best for the other, and competition isn't healthy. It needs to truly be half and half.

Step 3: When given the opportunity, present yourself to the media in a diplomatic and cooperative manner. If you're authentic and forthcoming, they'll know you're the real deal and a good source for future commentary on issues as they arise. If you choose not to respond to a question, rather than saying "*no comment,*" try this: "*I don't think I'm going to tell you that.*"

Step 4: If you are a parent or hope to be, stay aware of the affect of your Power Spouse™ role on your children. There are probably advantages in your lifestyle, but the children may not see it that way.

If you sense they resent being involved in certain public activities, be sensitive to their misgivings. *"Continue to nurture your own dreams and goals even as you care for your husband and children, especially during the teen years,"* says Ann Van De Water.[40]

Step 5: Nurture your own friendships carefully. Your friends don't need to be people your spouse knows, and sometimes it's better if he doesn't. Time spent with those who truly want the best for you is priceless.

Step 6: Make an effort to become familiar with the basics of his field. The purpose is not for you to actually take part, but for you to thrive next to him. There should be guidelines for events that involve your presence and a system must be in place for the exchange of information between home and the office. *"Since it is important to avoid missteps, you should find an experienced mentor or role model, just as any business would hire in the required expertise to fill in a gap,"* advises Rose Sheehan.[41]

Step 7: Pay attention to your health and wellness. Extra energy[42] is required to be a Power Spouse™. Special tip: At doctors' appointments, you can ask that you be called by your first name.

Step 8: Spend several hours a week doing what you enjoy. This is a key aspect of maintaining your individuality and helps to reduce any resentment you feel about spending time by his side at events.

Step 9: Make every effort to have as much solitude or privacy as you need. Call it *"me time"* or *"me parties."* This is essential to your peace of mind.

---

40   For advice on getting through those turbulent years, see Ann Van De Water's chapter 10.

41   In chapter 16, Rose Sheehan offers insights into various aspects of business that will help you be more comfortable as a Power Spouse™.

42   For specific tips on taking care of yourself, check out Barbara Anne Cookson's chapter 7.

Step 10: Say no to things that you don't want to do. That's easier said than done, but it's important in your efforts at time management. Identify the things you can enjoy that relate to his profession, then say no to those that you dislike. Set guidelines that deal with your participation; for example, require more than one day's notice for an event to make arrangements that include you.

Step 11: Demand and expect respect. Journalist Terry Pluto says, *"Home is where the 'hard' is."* Home is where we can be ourselves with those we love; however, sometimes the "public face" drains significant energy. Never accept less than the respect you deserve, and don't condone unacceptable behavior simply because it's happening in private.

Step 12: Develop ice-breaking conversation topics and questions. In the spotlight, your dinner partner often is someone other than your spouse. In this setting, it's appropriate to tell your story because you're getting acquainted with the person next to you. Two of my favorites are *"How did you meet [your spouse]?"* and *"Do you have pets?"*

Step 13: Develop patience and prudence. Using a deliberate pause before responding to what you may view as unreasonable or outrageous will go a long way toward maintaining restraint in your reactions. If you use social media, always be aware of its public aspect.

Step 14: Avoid being overly impressed by those who are successful in your husband's field of endeavor. The saying that "we all put on our pants one leg at a time" is key to remember. Meeting famous people is the same as encountering anyone else: Be friendly and you will gain more respect.

Step 15: Keep track of what you wore when annual or repeat events of any kind show up on your calendar. Then again, it's not the end of the world if you show up decked out in the same thing as you wore last year.

Step 16: Find a place to be anonymous. Being anonymous in a high-profile position is therapeutic. This is also good for your children. Once, on a beach vacation, my 10-year-old daughter said, *"Do you know what I like most about being on vacation?"* Her answer wasn't the surf, sand, or sun. *"People don't stare at us when we're here."*

Step 17: Practice smiling for a very long time. To convince me of the importance of this, my husband had a photo framed of me asking the person holding the camera, *"When are you going to take the picture?"* After seeing my facial contortions, I learned that I needed to "smile 'til it's stale."

Step 18: Make a conscious decision not to be stifled. Identify ways you've neglected yourself, whether it's your health, friendships, family time, or some area personal to you. Resolve to pay more attention to those aspects and you will feel better (and be a more valuable partner). Encourage conversations with your spouse so he understands how you feel. Enlist his help instead of allowing resentment to build up.

Do these steps really help you save your marriage and thrive in your husband's spotlight? Yes. I learned this the hard way, and that's why I'm sharing them with every woman who is stifled in the spotlight.

When you apply all 18 Steps to Power Spousing™, you will feel pride in your spouse and in yourself. Your relationship will improve while you thrive next to him. Your resentment will fade, and you'll keep your head above water in the fishbowl. You'll experience a heightened level of self-esteem and thrive.

Decide to UNstifle yourself and discover the rewards of shining in the spotlight as the woman you were meant to be. You deserve to thrive—and your family will be stronger as a result.

JOYCE SAWYER is the author of the groundbreaking book Power Spousing. A speaker, mentor, and advisor, she helps

women maintain their own identify when their spouse works in the spotlight of a high-profile profession. Learn more about Joyce in "Meet the Experts."

10

STRESS-LESS PARENTING

Ann Van De Water

T he WHACK! of the slammed door shook the house as the swearing tapered off. The silence was more deafening than the screaming, which seared her mother-heart with laserlike precision. Sophie and her daughter Clara[43] were very aware of the pain they had inflicted on each other. Both had become experts in knowing which buttons to push, which phrases to use, which wounds to inflict.

Their relationship had been crumbling for weeks as they prepared for Clara's departure for college. Both had said things they'd regretted and didn't mean, things like *"I can't stand you!"* Both had imagined things that weren't said at all and misinterpreted statements that came out badly. *"I have to get out of here!"* was a weekly echo in the halls of their home.

---

43 Names have been changed.

Clara was trying to spread her wings, and Sophie was holding on tighter than ever. Neither wanted to admit her part in the constant conflicts, and both were unaware of how their unexpressed stress over Clara's launch from the nest was playing a part in the electrified atmosphere in their home. Both treasured their relationship but were struggling with how to start to let go.

Have you ever been there? Can you relate to the searing pain? Have you ever reached a point in your parenting when you've lost hope and wondered if the love is salvageable? According to a research study,

> *"70 percent of young people say they have family support. Only 30 percent, however, felt they had positive family communication."* Furthermore, *"Positive family communication is much more common among younger kids than older teenagers; 47 percent of sixth graders report positive family communication, but only 22 percent of high school seniors do."*[44]

You are not alone. What you are experiencing is normal, and there are ways to break down the walls, no matter how long they've been building. Life with your child or even your young adult doesn't have to be like this! Do you realize that? Here's the rest of the story.

Sophie didn't know how to win Clara back and wondered what steps she could take to let her precious daughter know that she was loved unconditionally. At my recommendation as a parenting coach, Sophie started taking baby steps toward her daughter when she finally arrived as a freshman at her college dorm. These baby steps took the form of an invitation to lunch, a quick email asking how things were going, a pep talk text about Clara's college classes and the pressures she was feeling, a small gift dropped off at the dorm, a meal made and shared with Clara's roommates, a pin on Pinterest that showed

---

44 "Developmental Assets: A Profile of Your Youth" (Minneapolis: Search Institute, 2005), cited in "Family Communication: An Introduction," ParentFurther.com, http://www.parentfurther.com/parenting-matters/family-communication.

fun college room decor…little touch points that showed Clara that Sophie cared and was trying to reach out, to bridge the gap that had threatened to destroy their relationship.

As Sophie took these baby steps, Clara grew to see and appreciate her mother's heart. Once again, Sophie began to hear Clara's laughter, which had been missing for months in their home, as Clara began to drop in on weekends or come home for quick visits over the holidays. Sophie also began to smile again as well. Slowly, the wall was taken down, brick by brick, and they found their way back to each other.

It is so important to understand that there is *always* hope and, whether you realize it or not, life will often offer us second chances to have the relationships we want with the people we love. We just have to decide that we are willing to take the steps to make that happen. Lorraine Pursell says, *"It is the ability to apologize and humble ourselves before our kids that saves us."*[45]

So how can you do it? How can you break through to your child's or teen's heart and let them know that you want joy and peace in your household more than anything?

Begin with a plan. When there is no plan in place, you *react* instead of *respond*. Without a plan in place, you will find yourself doling out irrational, unfair, random consequences that are ineffective and cause more harm than good. However, there is a way to come out on the other end peacefully. Follow these steps.

6 Steps to Stress-Less Parenting

Step 1

The teenage years are characterized by what I call the 7 S's, and that's no way to live! *Determine which of the 7 S's you are dealing with*:

1. SCREAMING: out-of-control yelling (probably from both parties)

---

45 See Lorraine Pursell's chapter 11.

2. SOBBING: emotional meltdowns that sap all your energy and resolve and leave you spent
3. SILENCE: total communication breakdowns, including the cold shoulder
4. SWEARING: profanity that gets no one anywhere
5. SNEAKING: deceit, lying, and hidden agendas
6. SLAMMED DOORS: physical evidence of rage
7. SASS: need I really describe this to anyone?

Step 2

ZERO IN on the one *S* you want to target most. You have to take baby steps and tackle one thing at a time or nothing will get done. Warning: If you try to tackle too much at once, you will get frustrated, feel ineffective, and possibly end up with even more issues.

Chances are it may get worse before it gets better, but commit to seeing it through. Keep in mind the old adage *"You can't keep doing the same thing and expect things to change!"*

Step 3

IDENTIFY how you feel. Realize that it's important to acknowledge those feelings and that it's normal and okay to experience them! Know that you need to take steps for a healthier you, emotionally and psychologically, to recover from the battering that unhealthy relationships or devastating circumstances can cause. Life can and will throw us curveballs. That is guaranteed. Know that no matter what you have experienced, you can change the way things are.

Step 4

EXPRESS calmly your desire to turn things around and make things different—first to yourself, and then to your young adult. Help them understand that this will take a team effort and that you have to start on the same page with an understanding. Discuss your goals and the steps you each must take to improve the current situation.

Step 5

DECIDE on the one new behavior you wish to see instead from your young adult and be open to the possibility that you may have to do some things differently as well to achieve your desired results.

As Marilyn Ida Horowitz reminds us, *"Increased awareness of events (or situations) in your past that helped to profoundly influence something in your life today can help you gain a greater understanding of yourself (and your relationships) by connecting your present with your past."* [46]

Consider this as you move forward.

Step 6

BEGIN TODAY to take some of those baby steps I mentioned earlier toward a new relationship and celebrate the small victories as they come on the way to your ultimate success. Think of others that would be particularly powerful in your particular situation. You are limited only by your own creativity in thinking of special way to connect again. Angela Alexander reminds us, *"The miracle is in the action!"* [47]

It's never too late to plan and implement a healthier course of action to turn things around in your home or in your life with your adult children. We do get second chances, and the 6 Steps to Stress-Less Parenting will help you with your children no matter what their age.

Just as our children can wear us out and break us down, we can break through to them with constant and persistent communication. It may appear not to be working with the first few attempts, but stick with it! Make sure they know you're not giving up! Get stubborn and decide that you are committed to a stress-less environment in your home.

---

46   See Marilyn Ida Horowitz's chapter 8.
47   See Angela Alexander's chapter 12.

Picture yourself in a more peaceful place than you are now. Know and accept that you are in this for the long haul and that the unhampered expression of unconditional love will make all the difference. Above all, maintain a sense of humor—it will go a long way toward lightening up even the most stressful situations!

This may all seem impossible from where you sit right now, but I assure you that what you have experienced from your young adult is the outward evidence of inward struggles and that it can dissipate with honest communication and expression of unconditional love and support.

Stay strong and be assured of your role as parent in all situations. Your confidence will speak volumes as you lead with love. [48]

Steps You Can Take Now

- Zero in on one thing you want to see changed,
- Identify how you feel,
- Express your desire to turn things around,
- Decide on one new behavior you wish to see,
- Commit to changing your own responses to the status quo, and
- Begin today to take baby steps.

I've seen miracles happen with my clients, and I know it can work. If you will take the first few baby steps in the right direction, you could experience an amazing, life-giving breakthrough, not only for yourself, but for your young adult.

When it comes right down to it, don't we all desire peace and loving relationships in our homes? Can we picture our children when they are around 30 years old as happy, healthy, loving, caring, responsible adults? Can we focus on the goal of launching them from the nest with the values, skills, and morals that will help them to become contributing, compassionate, and successful members of society? Can we commit to taking the baby steps necessary to reach

---

48 See Joyce Sawyer's chapter 9 for tips on maintaining your own identity while raising children who demand your time and attention.

those goals and revel in the fact that sometimes what we think are fairy tales just might come true?

Can you dare to hope for a home filled with peace and unconditional love? Is it possible to tear down the walls and rebuild the war-torn relationship with your young adult? Will you dare to dream of days ahead that will find you in a meaningful friendship with your adult child?

I pray your answer is yes!

ANN VAN DE WATER is a wife, mother, grandmother, and published author of a humorous collection of anecdotes about mothering titled *Mommy Memoirs: A Hilarious and Heartwarming Look at the Trials and Triumphs of Being a Mom.* She and her husband, Wes, are Certified Leadership Parenting Coaches through the John Rosemond Institute. Learn more about Ann in "Meet the Experts."

›11‹

4-F FORMULA MOTHERING

Lorraine Pursell, MA

I couldn't stop yelling at him. There he was, only four years old. What could he have possibly done to warrant my behavior?

He was huddled on the floor in the hallway to protect himself from me, yet he would peek his head around the corner to see me, as if he loved me so much that he could not stay away.

When I finally got hold of myself I went to him, my heart broken in a million pieces. What had I done to my boy?

I crouched down, put my hand gently on his back and asked, "*Mark, how do you feel right now?*"

In his quiet little voice, he said, "*I feel afraid of you.*"

Oh. "*What do you feel afraid of?*" I asked.

"*I'm afraid of you because I don't know what you are going to do.*"

Déjà vu washed over me as my four-year-old son articulated my childhood—this is exactly how I felt growing up: Were my parents

72

going to be nice or mean, loving or raging? And there I was, though I'd determined not to repeat my parents' mistakes, behaving just like them.

You Are Not Alone

Have you found yourself in similar situations? You are not alone.

"Yelling at children is so common in American households that most parents view it as an inevitable part of childrearing," says the *New York Times.*[49]

We all know how it starts: stress. Life is stressful, especially in the 21st century, and it is easy to attack those closest to us. After all, no one is closer to us than our children.

"88 percent of parents say they've shouted or screamed at their kids in the previous year (the figure shoots up to 98 percent of parents with 7-year-olds and 56 percent of mothers of 4-year-olds yell in anger at least once or twice a week)."[50]

The effect of yelling at our kids is this: Children who are yelled at and verbally abused are at risk for depression in teen years.

It Can Change

Before I became a marriage, family, and child counselor, I helped myself. You see, the opening story is mine. That dreadful night when my son cowered on the floor, I vowed to be the best parent I could possibly be. I went into therapy for years, created and followed the 4-F Formula™ to make sure my relationship with my child was as I wanted it, and Mark's and my relationship flourished. In fact, it still does 30 years later.

I discovered that it is very possible to turn family misery into family harmony. The following four simple steps will work for you like they have for me, and for the past 19 years in my clients' lives.

---

49 Bonnie Rothman Morris, "Scream at Your Own Risk (and Your Children's)," *New York Times*, November 9, 2004.

50 Jeannie Ralston, "How to Curb Your Anger," Parenting.com, http://www. parenting.com/article/how-to-curb-your-anger.

Here is the 4-F Formula™ that you can use to change your family for the better forever.

1. Face Up

When we escalate and yell, we actually enter a hypnotic state triggered by something in our past that we have not yet faced or healed from. We go unconscious, like I did in 1984. For me, that night was a mix of being scared about leaving my ex-husband and feeling incapable of raising a four-year-old while dealing with my own problems. When I looked further, I saw that I reenacted my mother's responses. As a child, my mother was usually stressed about wanting to leave her unhappy marriage. Because of this, she didn't know how to handle the pressure of raising four kids simultaneously and often took her stress out on the kids. And while I understood her frustration, when I saw that I was repeating her errors, it was what drove me to change. That's your step 1: face up.

When we face the fact that we have a yelling or anger problem, we muster great courage. Our bravery continues as we recall and examine our own childhood each time we have a knee-jerk yelling response—the reaction that springs from our lips, or hands if we hit, with surprise and no premeditation. From now on, each time you yell ask yourself, *"When have I felt this before?"*[51] and *"How old do I feel right now?"* This one process will lead you to the root of your trouble and point you in the right direction. Further, it is the way to self-realization and the crystal clarity of self-healing.

Breathing is important here. Deeply inhale and exhale at least three strong breaths to break your trance. Notice the uncomfortable sensations in your body. Where do you feel anxiety, nervousness, or anger—in your chest, arms, head, legs, or gut? Are your ears hot? Your body faithfully signals when you're heading for trouble, so stop and take care of yourself right away. Noticing your body and those

---

51   Marilyn Ida Horowitz gives us a fantastic tool to help us sort through our triggers, those things that we do without thinking and usually deeply regret later. Read her chapter 8 to uncover and examine the first times you felt your uneasy feelings.

early warning signs gives you a chance to regroup and gain composure before you do something you will regret later.

2. Fess Up

Go to your children. Tell them you have made a terrible mistake and that you are sorry. When you humble yourself you take a stand for your change, and your children see an example of what to do in their own lives. This step is vital. In fact, your sincere apology is the magic that fuels this 4-F Formula™.

Often, the mantle of mothering brings with it the feeling that we should have all the answers about mothering. There is no way that birthing a baby equips us for what lies ahead. Sure, a lot of mother instinct kicks in, but knowing the all right answers for our children as they grow? Unlikely. Except for trusting our gut and going with our intuition, we have nothing to lean on but how we were raised. And actually, having a child fosters insecurity within us. We seem to realize—maybe for the first time—how lost we actually feel!

No one automatically knows how to parent, and it's okay to admit that. Come clean with your children. Let them know that you make mistakes every day. When we sincerely apologize and even ask what we can do to make it up to them, they see a real person they can trust and an example for avoiding perfectionist pitfalls in their own lives.

Fess up to yourself, too. Look into your own eyes in your bathroom mirror. You were triggered by unresolved pain in your childhood. Say to yourself, *"I love you. I am doing my best, and I will get better. I will be gentle with me."* Then embrace that abandoned part of you that got left behind when you were little. Ask your own inner child what she needs from you. Let her crawl into your lap and hug and hold her until her anguish is soothed. Each time you do this you will get closer to your own healing.

3. Firm Up

Ask your children for help. Create a signal with your children and give them permission to use it when they notice you escalating, such as hearing your voice raise or seeing an angry look on your face. Promise that you won't be angry at them for pointing this out to you. Make sure they feel safe to help you, or they won't. This will bring you closer to your children because you are asking for their assistance. And this step builds a bridge between your hearts; as you practice this step, you create a lasting, lifelong bond so your children want to spend time with you after they leave your nest. They will feel important as they help co-architect their upbringing. As they become your partners you are taking giant steps in the right direction!

Ann Van De Water says, *"If parents learn to forgive and ask for forgiveness on our journey, we not only receive the gift of second chances, but model for our children those important concepts."* [52]

Your children will learn that they are not always to blame when you get angry. As you share openly with them, they learn to understand you and see that you are doing your best, just as your own parents did. Now that you have your own kids, you can see the whole picture differently.

4. Free Up

The last step is to watch and experience these first three steps revolutionize and transform your family and your child's self-esteem. As we grow, we become a whole person and more capable of raising children. Your willingness to admit when you are wrong and change is love in action. You drop the know-it-all mother persona and become someone who needs your children's help. Who better than them to advise you on your mothering journey?

Vulnerable leadership, the ability to admit one's errors, is powerful. When we parent with openness, we elicit respect from our kids that otherwise would be lost in anger. I asked my own child many times what he needed from me as a parent. Those conversations

52   See Ann Van De Water's chapter 10.

brought rich insights into the inner workings of my son. As I listened and acted on his suggestions, his love and respect for me grew.

I remember the day Mark made me promise not to get angry before he told me some upsetting news. This set a precedent for us—I swallowed hard and paused long until I found a place deep within me, then honored him by keeping my promise. Our communication and honesty grew greatly through the years because he felt safe and I gained control of my emotions.

Barbara Cookson says, *"When we incorporate the valuable opinions of our children in their upbringing, we not only parent well, but we give them an indelible sense of their self-worth."*[53]

I know you can do this. Your reward will be your children's lifelong endearment and wanting to spend time with you when they no longer have to, long after they have left home.

There Is More

Thanks to the 4-F Formula™ my story gets better. Last spring my son called me and said, *"Mom, I would love nothing more than for you to come and be a part of my family."*

I packed up my Jeep, shipped it from the Big Island of Hawai'i where I lived at the time, and drove across the United States to be with them.

As I finish this chapter, two of my three grandkids are visiting me and telling me about their fun and fantastic days. This is irreplaceable and a future I wish for you.

We don't go through the tears, toils, and joys of motherhood only to have our kids want to stay away after they leave at 18.

This system works. Follow the 4-F Formula™ and get the family you want.

LORRAINE PURSELL, MA, holds a master's degree in marriage, family, and child counseling and coaches through private practice, writing, radio, and speaking. She specializes in

---

53   See Barbara Anne Cookson's chapter 7.

private one-on-one retreats for individuals, couples, and families to help them attain happy lives and relationships. Learn more about Lorraine in "Meet the Experts."

12

TURN PAIN INTO POWER AND GRIEF INTO PEACE

Angela Alexander

Special report: *An African American women was found deceased in her Lakewood apartment early this morning.*

My body turned to ice. My blood instantly drained from my head to my soles. Even without hearing her name, I knew he was talking about my sister.

For months, my nightly dreams were unbearable, replaying every detail I tried to block out. The pain was raw and real. I couldn't think clearly or walk straight. I drove aimlessly.

I felt like I'd been hit by a freight train, like I'd survived with every nerve left opened and exposed to be wounded again at will. I was lost mentally, spiritually, and emotionally. A year passed before I could say the words out loud.

"Alice is dead."

As the words came out, I felt my heart break into a million little pieces.

The death of my sister was excruciatingly painful and made worse when people said, *"I know how you feel."*

I knew they meant well, but they didn't have a clue! If they truly knew how I felt they would have called 911 and had me admitted and committed; as Zig Ziglar said, I seriously needed a *"checkup from the neck up."*

What I Learned

Grief is filled with pain, and your pain is real whether you're dealing with the death of your loved one, the end of your marriage, the foreclosure of your home, or difficult losses in your career health, wealth, or dreams. We all experience pain and grief in multiple areas of our lives, and the resolution is to discover how to turn our pain into power and our grief into peace.

To be angry with yourself, others, or even your God is natural. Talking about your grief definitely helps; however, harping on it to the point where you become bitter is unhealthy.

Invite people to listen to you, but know that misery loves company. However, that doesn't mean you have to RSVP and upgrade to VIP status.

Ann Van De Water says, *"One can get a sense of peace in dealing with their emotions, admitting the pain, realizing that they will experience the whole spectrum of feelings and that is normal. Bitterness, anger, grief, and depression are all emotions that will appear in the course of a lifetime full of relationships and painful losses . . . but to nurse the pain is a curse."* [54]

Would your loved ones want you to be miserable day after day? Remember: The healing of your broken heart is not an indication that you no longer love or miss them.

---

54 See Ann Van De Water's chapter 10.

Four years after my sister passed I was in Japan on military duty. I was summoned to a small office, where a priest was nervously holding paperwork from the Red Cross. He informed me that my husband and four children had been in a horrific car crash.

"Your husband, Surie, he's in the hospital, but he's okay.
"Your daughter Angela, she's in the hospital, but she's okay.
"Your daughter Angelina, she's in the hospital, but she's okay.
"Your two eight-year-old sons, Murice and Roger, they didn't make it."

I recalled a prayer my children said before going to bed.

Now I lay me down to sleep,
I pray the Lord my soul to keep.
If I should die before I wake,
I pray the Lord my soul to take.

I wanted to hear my sons' voices. I felt them in my heart and I heard them say, *"No, Mommy, that priest is wrong. We prayed the Lord our soul to take and we did make it. We're here!"*

Instantly I felt a sense of peace—there was no room for pain. The people in the room were watching and waiting for my world to turn upside down. Instead, they found me at ease.

The journey I'd traveled and the lessons I'd learned all prepared me for such a time as this. Many times I have heard and read about that peace that passes all understanding; however, I never experienced that version of peace until this moment, when my personal faith took over and helped me through the one thing I thought I would never have to face: the passing of my children.

It All Begins with Faith and Service

Faith is personal, and it isn't my goal to tell you what to believe. I do want to encourage you to find your own version of faith and then bring it deeply into your life. Start now, before you need it, so it will be there for you when you do.

April 1, 2000, the day my sons passed, was the day my faith was revealed, not built. However, it all begins with faith and service.

With your talents or gifts, how can you serve others? When you're helping others, an unexpected blessing takes place as your pain turns into power and grief into peace.

When disaster struck my family we continued to serve as foster parents and learned that when you have a great pain you need to have a greater purpose. During your time of grief search for the miracles and focus on what you're grateful for. What you think about you bring about.

I've learned that death is inevitable, but misery is optional. Now, what excites your soul? Will grief be the obstacle that prevents you from living fully, on purpose, with excitement, passion, and a zest for life? I'm simply asking you, are your dreams planted or buried?

7 Steps from Grief to Peace

Step 1: Find Your Faith, Whatever It May Be, and Pray in the Way That Feels Best to You for Help Healing Your Broken Heart

- Prayers changes things. Your words don't have to be eloquent; simply speak from your heart.
- Know that it's okay to ask for help.

Step 2: Express Gratitude

- Focus on what you're grateful for throughout your day, and write down five good things daily.
- There is good in this world. I truly believe that statement remains true even on your darkest day.
- Search for and share your miracles.

Step 3: Forgive

Forgiveness is simply mandatory for your sanity. It will set you free. This freedom will release your thoughts, giving you more energy to heal your broken heart. What you want, you should give. Be the blessing you would like to receive. What you sow, you'll reap. You can't hold back forgiveness and expect to be forgiven.

Forgiveness doesn't mean the other person right or you are wrong. Would you rather be right or righteous? When we don't forgive we stay in pain longer than we need to stay, and pay a greater cost than we need to pay. Don't self-sabotage by holding on to your pain. Instead, be transformed by the renewal of your mind. Lewis Smedes says, *"To forgive is to set a prisoner free and discover that the prisoner was you."* [55]

It's been expressed that the love you withhold is the pain you carry. Lesley Graham says, *"Grief and unforgiveness left untreated can develop into chronic illnesses."* [56]

Step 4: Write a Letter to Your Loved One

- Say good-bye if you didn't get a chance to.
- Ask for, give, or receive forgiveness if needed.
- Read and add to your letter as you desire.

Step 5: Listen to Inspirational Music

- Music is therapeutic, helpful, and healing.
- Write the lyrics down and reflect on the message.

Step 6: Take a Daily Walk, or Exercise

Getting out of the house will help you from becoming isolated, withdrawn, or homebound. Barbara Anne Cookson confirms, *"Exercising causes a release of endorphins (those feel-good chemicals) from your brain, which actually can make you feel happier."* [57]

---

55 Lewis B. Smedes, *Forgive and Forget: Healing the Hurts We Don't Deserve* (New York: Harper, 1984).
56 See Lesley Graham's chapter 14.
57 See Barbara Anne Cookson's chapter 7.

Step 7: Attend Individual or Group Grief Counseling Sessions

Fellowshipping with other believers who are grieving could be extremely beneficial, especially if they are further along in their grief process. Some may be living the peace you desire to achieve.

Things will never be the same again; however, the passing of your loved one doesn't have to be the worst thing that ever happened to you if you don't allow it.

Do you want to enjoy life and be there for your friends' and family's gatherings, weddings, graduations, holidays, vacations, etc.? If so I encourage you to apply the *7 Steps from Grief to Peace* in your daily routine.

If your dreams are buried, just imagine what will happen if you take action by watering them daily with your faith, hopes, and visions for a brighter future. You reap what you sow, what you give. Plant seeds of love, generosity, and prosperity!

You were created to be powerful, not pitiful. Life is about choices. The power is within you to make a difference, beginning with yourself, right now. Think about how your life could change if you allowed the 7 steps to take place? The transformation is gradual but necessary to fulfill the desires of your heart.

After my sister passed I was extremely depressed, confused, and lonely for way too long. I was truly trippin' and my mind had gone skinny-dippin'! During that time I learned that love never dies.

When my sons passed I applied these 7 steps, and my healing process was much healthier, my mind was at ease, and I looked forward to the future. Because of this tranquility many people continue to think I have great closure. Not true. I'll have closure when I see my loved ones again, but what I do have is peace on earth.

How do you turn your grief into good grief? You turn your hurt into your harvest, your pain into your power, your power into your passion, that mess into your message, your situation into your sanctuary, your test into your testimony, your worries into your worship, and your misery into your miracles.

ANGELA ALEXANDER retired from the Air Force Reserve and is now an inspirational speaker and the author of her autobiography, titled *Miracles in Action*. God allowed Angela to transform what could have easily devastated her and her family's lives forever into a ministry that blesses all who hear this incredible testimony. Learn more about Angela in "Meet the Experts."

13

LIVING YOUR LIFE WITH PURPOSE

Barry Laub, MS, CFP

I don't know what to do. I am making plenty of money, I live in a great house, and I have the ideal family that other people wish they had. Why am I scared? Why do I have the feeling that it will all crumble? Why am I so stressed? What should I do? Should I go after the promotion that will give me more money? The downside is that I will have even less time than I have now. I can't afford to change careers, yet I want to feel more satisfied and enthusiastic about my life and career. I am so confused!

If you're too busy to be happy or feel there ought to be more meaning to your life, then all of that probably sounds very familiar to you.

The good news is you're not alone. As a business coach, I meet professionals every day who wrestle with similar issues regardless of the level they have achieved or the industry they are in.

They want their life to have more meaning. They are bored doing the same job year after year. Money doesn't take the place of meaning, yet they can't quit because they have developed a lifestyle with expenses that have to be paid.

They hide their dissatisfaction for fear people won't understand. But you understand, don't you?

When your passion or life purpose is not active, it's inevitable that you'll feel lost. The solution is different for everyone, and there is a solution no matter what your situation.

For some it is being reinvigorated with a hobby or an activity. Others move on to a new career.

Whatever the issue, the first step is to recognize you are not a prisoner of circumstances.

The second step is to know you're not alone. Experiencing a lack of purpose is very common. Let's look at what to do if this is where you are.

In 2013, a Gallup poll found that 40% of Americans have not found a satisfying life purpose. If you are one of the 40%, it is now time to address your desire to get in touch with your life purpose.

Sadly, life purpose is never addressed in school, and most likely your business life has been about making money. The less you are involved with feeling that you are living and working with a purpose that will leave a lasting legacy, the more likely you will question why you are doing what you are doing.

There are times when we feel helpless, as if there were nothing we can do for ourselves. The way to beat this is by finding a larger cause in helping others. By thinking about how we can make it better for other people, we create a mission for ourselves and get unstuck.

Living your life with purpose begins with your mindset. What you tell yourself is your only truth. When you change the story and develop a different set of beliefs, this will become your new truth and your new way of seeing the life that you are living.

You do not have to change your career or leave your job. Your mindset and attitude can change, which will in turn change your state of mind. You can look at a different job or career that will be more fulfilling.

Many of my clients found their fear was holding them back from getting what they wanted. Perhaps that's you, too. Sometimes fear around losing money keeps us from making changes. When we adjust the facts and listen to different messages, we can minimize the fear and then progress to a more satisfying life.

The secret is to realize that you create the stories you hear in your head. When you see that, then you can begin to find your purpose. When you understand that you create your reality, then you can accept that you are in charge of rewriting your life now and making it what you'd like it to be.

Are you ready to say *"enough is enough"*?

Helen was an audit partner in a prominent accounting firm. She was hoping to be promoted to equity partner. When she was passed over for this opportunity she felt that enough was enough. The commute back and forth from her home added three hours a day of travel time. Being a full-time professional and the mother of two small children is a very challenging task. The firm was paying her very well for her position, and she feared that she would not receive the same compensation someplace else. Helen was the primary breadwinner for her family. This was a real dilemma for Helen. She was exhausted, unfulfilled, and scared to make a move. However, she knew she could no longer go on like this.

There is no one right solution for everybody. The solution is to wake up every morning feeling grateful and satisfied that you are fulfilling your life's purpose.

Helena Nyman, The Executive Champion Maker, says, *"Purpose magnifies your success. You are the champion of your decisions."* [58]

So what decisions will you make today?

Helen decided to contact a headhunter. She let the headhunter know she wanted a shorter commute and comparable compensation. She was not looking for another position in auditing. Helen started

---

58   See Helena Nyman's chapter 4.

to go on interviews to see if there was an alternative. She also spoke to some of her contacts. Six weeks later she was offered a job as a chief operating officer for another company with a commute of only 80 minutes per day with fewer hours than she was working before.

Barbara Cookson, an accomplished empowerment coach, shares, *"When one lives their life with purpose, happiness is inevitable."* [59]

What is the happiness you are seeking?

You too can be fulfilled, satisfied, and grateful to be living the life you desire. Just like Helen, when you change your mindset to overcome fear and embrace possibilities, different doors will open up for you.

Helen is now teaching and training other employees as part of her role. She has never been happier with a job. Helen is now making a difference in the lives of others in a way that she finds very rewarding.

Happiness can be yours when you stop tolerating what you do not want and uncover what it is that energizes you.

Steven Sanchez, an Internet development expert, shared with me, *"As I guide my children into adulthood, my advice is not to choose the course that will make them rich. No, when all the choices are weighed, the 'right' choice is to live life with purpose, on purpose."* [60]

As you can see, these experts all share one thing in common: Purpose is the element that is the deciding factor for one to achieve true happiness and fulfillment.

So are you ready to achieve fulfillment by finding your life purpose? Follow these simple steps.

5 Steps to Achieving Fulfillment by Finding Your Life Purpose

Step 1

Ask family and friends who know you well what they believe drives you the most in helping others. As they answer your question, pay

---

59   See Barbara Anne Cookson's chapter 7.
60   See Steven Sanchez's chapter 5.

close attention to what they say and you will find your why—the purpose you were put on this planet to fulfill.

Step 2

Create a plan to live your purpose. According to Rita Ferguson, an expert in project management, *"Working the plan or executing the plan is key. Execution breathes life into your purpose and infuses energy into you. That's when the magic happens!"* [61]

So sit down and map out your plan to discover and live your life's purpose—then follow your plan.

Step 3

Ask yourself one question: What would you like to be remembered for? Visualize your funeral and the eulogy delivered about you.

Sit down in a quiet space where you will not be interrupted. Gather your thoughts and just start writing whatever comes to mind about how you would like to be remembered. When you finish, you will have the purpose for all that you do. Once you know what you want to be known for, you can design the implementation of your actions around this purpose.

Step 4

Find someone who can assist you to support your purpose and mission to find fulfillment. It's critical that you choose someone who will not advise you based on his or her own beliefs, prejudices, likes, and dislikes. This person must have the capacity to listen and even advise you when you need it, all in service of helping you get what you want. No one achieves life purpose or fulfillment alone.

Step 5

Once you have found your purpose and are beginning to experience the joys of fulfillment, be on the lookout for the signs that say you

---

61   See Rita Ferguson's chapter 6.

might not be living your purpose fully and completely. If you're tired, depressed, bored, or scared, or feeling a sense of being lost in your own life, seek guidance to find your way back. Once you understand precisely what you're meant to do, nothing will stop you from achieving it.

Do not allow your fears around making a living to prevent you from imagining possibilities. When you want something more than what is holding you back, the choice will become easier to make. Please do not allow your fears to prevent the legacy you so deserve.

Ultimately, the act of making a difference for others is your greatest reward. It brings joy and incredible fulfillment. You can have it if you decide that you deserve more in life than your current condition, regardless of how much or little money that you are making. You're worth it!

Decide now to Live Your Life With Purpose!

BARRY LAUB, MS, CFP, is a number one bestselling author dedicated to impacting individuals in fulfilling their life purpose. He is known as an engaging speaker and a master of mindset and attitude. He has been called a business, career, and life visionary providing empowerment to all who encounter him. Learn more about Barry in "Meet the Experts."

14

STAND UP AND TAKE CHARGE

Lesley Graham, RN

As she entered the accident and emergency area of the hospital, she was losing her ability to stay conscious. The pain was excruciating, the overwhelming tiredness was taking her, she was unable to think straight, and she was struggling to stay coherent.

Just the day before she had returned from a trip on the west coast of Ireland, where she had spent a glorious week communing with a group of women from around the world who were seeking out ancient myths on a journey of awakening.

Guided by a local Irishman, they had walked through villages by ancient sites and shared stories of myths and legends. Then, while descending down a mountain, she tried to steady herself by grabbing a clump of heather and noticed a black insect shaped like an arrowhead attached to her wrist. She flicked it off and continued down the mountainside, unaware that her life was about to change forever.

A few days later she found herself curled up in bed with a pillow over her head trying to keep out the light. Her whole body was burning up and in pain. She needed desperately to go to the bathroom. However, earlier attempts to climb out of bed had been a struggle.

Unable to escape from the discomfort in her bladder and piercing pain in her head, she placed both feet on the floor and instantly doubled over, losing her balance and lurching forward toward the chest of drawers and door handle.

Fortunately, the door swung open and her daughter appeared.

Within an hour they were at the hospital, where a young doctor arrived to carry out the initial medical assessment. After a plethora of questions, he scratched his head, baffled. He went to discuss her case with his colleagues, warning her it would be quite a wait.

She had no idea how true that would come to be.

Days and weeks went by with no diagnosis. Excruciating pain, muscle spasms, spiking temperatures at night, and icy cold during the day plagued her. Even standing up was a major operation. Weeks led to months, and she lost her ability to work.

It was nearly a year before a doctor finally diagnosed her with Lyme disease, caused by bacteria transmitted to humans via the bite of an infected tick or blood-feeding insect. The condition can be fatal, as it can affect all major organs, bones, muscles, eyesight, and brain function.

Seven to 10 days after a bite by an infected insect, the first stage of Lyme disease begins with flu-like symptoms—fever, chills, swollen lymph nodes, headaches, fatigue, muscle fatigue, and joint pains.

Neurological complications most often occur in the second stage of Lyme. These include numbness, pain, weakness, visual disturbances, and meningitis symptoms such as stiff neck and severe headache. Left undiagnosed, problems such as difficulty concentrating, irritability, depression, fatigue, muscle pain, memory, sleep disorders, and nerve damage may occur.

Though the doctor had diagnosed her disease, he was unable to cure her. She was unable to stand for more than a few minutes, and her feet were raw and burning with every step. Her balance was off, and excruciating cramps in her legs at night meant very little sleep. This led to extreme changes in her ability to think logically, recall information within minutes of receiving it, or figure out simple math.

Life was no longer normal.

"There is nothing we can do," the doctors told her.

Frustrated, overwhelmed, anxious, and depressed, she looked up at the sky and asked, *"Please someone help me."*

She suddenly remembered words she had read long ago: *"If you change the way you look at things, the things you look at change"*[62] and *"The starting point of all achievement is desire."*[63]

So there it was. Desire was key, and she had that in spades. She wanted her life back.

Others who had recovered from life-threatening illnesses advised her to start not with what doctors tell you but with what they don't tell you.

Katerina St. Claire says, *"Stepping up and taking charge of your health is as simple as a prayer and forming an intention to heal your body."*[64]

It was time to stand up, take charge, and accept nothing less than complete healing. She was on her way and soon discovered that what the doctors don't tell you can help you recover—even from illnesses they say can't be cured.

Here's what she learned.

---

62   Wayne Dyer.
63   Napoleon Hill, *Think and Grow Rich* (Meriden, CT: Ralston Society, 1937).
64   See Katerina St. Claire's chapter 15.

5 Simple Steps to Stand Up and Take Charge of Your Health

Step 1: LOVE Thyself, Know Your Own Limitations,
Stand Up, and Take Charge

The reality is that the body can heal itself. We all have a natural healing mechanism in the body. This is well known and taught in medical school. We all make cancer cells, viruses, and bacteria every day, and our body fights them every day.

These natural healing mechanisms operate only when the nervous system is in the relaxation response. The autonomic nervous system, which regulates involuntary functions, is comprised of two parts: (1) the sympathetic, which is your "fight or flight" stress response, and (2) the parasympathetic, your relaxation response. It is with the latter that the body flips into its natural healing mechanism.

But in our modern culture, people's bodies are, on average, in a stress response 50 times a day! Worse, every time we are in stress response our healing mechanisms are turned off.

What is needed is a combination of a nurturing belief and positive care with a healer who really matters for you, one you truly believe and trust, one who takes you into his or her arms and says, *"You're not alone anymore. I'm here with you. We are going to get through this together."*

This powerful communication relaxes the nervous system and drops into the parasympathetic nervous system, and the good feeling mechanism gets switched on. The body starts taking care of itself again.

Step 2: EXERCISE Gently

Move gently at first,[65] 15 minutes a day if you can. If not, start with five minutes a day and build up.

---

65   Do not engage in any exercise regimen unless you are cleared to do so by a competent physician.

- Begin by stretching your arms and legs, rotating your wrists one way and then the other, and repeat with your ankles.
- Move your head from side to side, go for short and then longer walks, and increase your distance by even a few steps weekly.
- If swimming is easier to support your body, do that. Even 15 minutes of gentle movement in the water can release the tension in your body.
- Know your limitations and take it slowly.

Step 3: Pay Attention to Your MIND Talk

Your problem isn't the problem. Your reaction is the problem.[66] Don't come from the place that you're broken and need fixing. Get support. Consider coaching and attend workshops. You don't have to do this alone. Consider, for instance, anomalous healing or mind-body medicine, a concept that has long been practiced by the indigenous Q'ero people in Peru, who are the longest-living people in the world.

As Certified Holistic Health Coach and motivational speaker Barbara Anne Cookson says, *"When the mind and the body are out of balance, this can lead to ill health."*

She advises that you ask yourself these questions:

- What might lie at the root of your illness that might be out of alignment with the truth in your life?
- What is your body saying no to?
- What does your body need in order to heal?[67]

See where the answers are related to your lifestyle, your job, or your relationships. Then work on healing these areas.

---

66 As Joyce Sawyer says, *"You're better off not thinking about your condition; it will only make it worse if you do."* See chapter 9.

67 See Barbara Anne Cookson's chapter 7.

Step 4: Recognize That OPPORTUNITIES Don't Happen— You Create Them

Read the latest research on your condition. Don't just accept the diagnosis and test results. Look for alternatives. Keep a daily journal with your findings, visualize how you want to see yourself in the future, and put it out to the universe for help.

Research on spontaneous remission says there are 35,000 medical reports of people who had stage 4 cancer, heart disease, thyroid disease, diabetes, and autoimmune disorders **and have had spontaneous remissions**.

Yes, this leads to the question of the placebo effect. In medical school it is well known and documented that the placebo effect exists. This phenomenon was discovered as a side effect of pharmaceutical trials used to determine if a new drug was effective and better than giving someone a sugar pill. Results found that often people would have remission or resolution of their symptoms as a result of this fake treatment. Therefore, can the body heal itself? Yes. This is proof positive.

Step 5: Adjust Your NUTRITION

The key to helping your body heal itself is to be careful about what you put into your body. Look online for a qualified nutritionist in your area and ask for an "individual holistic assessment." Most importantly, eat healthy meals little and often. If your appetite is low, consider soups or smoothies.

Do these steps seem too simple? Is it really possible to heal from disease that doctors say can't be cured? **The answer is absolutely *yes*!**

How do I know? The story I've shared with you about the woman with Lyme disease is my own. The 5 Steps I've given you are precisely how I got my life back.

I've seen the 5 Steps work for many others as well. In fact, I've been a nurse for 40 years and have looked after many patients along the way. I've witnessed many miracles—patients getting back their lives against all odds with sheer determination and the 5 Steps.

I've seen alternative approaches pay off where traditional medicine let them down. I am trained in traditional medicine—and I'm telling you to look elsewhere. What does that tell you?

As I write the final words to this chapter, I am sitting in Willka T'ika—a spiritual retreat in Peru. I just completed walking three hours up a mountain track in the Sacred Valley at a very high altitude and I feel great. It has taken nearly three years for me to reach this point with no medical intervention whatsoever. Now I am pain-free and able to walk long distances and live a normal life.

It would have taken a lot less time if I'd known earlier how to activate the five steps I've shared with you, and now I've devoted the rest of my life to making sure everyone knows what I've learned—that we all need to stand up and take charge of our own health.

Start now so you never have to waste one moment of your life.

LESLEY GRAHAM, RN, is a specialist nurse, coach, Reiki master, and founder of Stand Up and Take Charge. She has worked in the National Health Service in the north of England for 40 years and retired in 2012 due to a life-threatening illness. Having now made a remarkable recovery, she shares her story. Learn more about Lesley in "Meet the Experts."

⟩15⟨

DISCOVER YOUR HIDDEN POWER USING QUANTUM MEDICINE

Katerina St. Claire

In my work as an energy healer, I have seen many miracles. Men and women who were left for dead from severe stokes and near-fatal accidents miraculously recovered to live normal lives.

Is this "woo-woo," or is it science? My teachers[68] say energy healing finds its foundation in quantum physics and mechanics and is accomplished by *setting the intention of healing the health of my clients and patients by prayer and focus.*

That's when miraculous healings occur.

---

68 Brilliant healers associated with the International Quantum University of Integrative Medicine, the American Holistic Medical Association, Quantum-Touch, Healing Beyond Borders, and many others.

Science has shown that all things are vibrating from the subatomic, atomic, molecular, cellular, organ, and body levels, including our outer energy fields, which scientists have named auras. The universe is in constant motion all the time and subatomic theories are being proven every day.

When the Higgs boson was proven to be a real subatomic energy particle, an influencer similar to gravity, it gave creditability to other subatomic theories.

Lesley Graham says, *"When you tap into universal energy, a whole new way of living opens up."*[69]

Epigenetics is one of the fastest growing subatomic theories and addresses DNA influencers. Epigenetics explains how identical twins with identical DNA can have different personalities, strengths, and weaknesses. By removing *baggage* DNA or epigenetic *splinter* influences, significant physical, emotional, and mental changes can result in positive outcomes.

Perhaps you've heard the stories about individuals miraculously recovering after being prayed for in a prayer circle or after hands-on healing by an energy practitioner.

Can science explain these healings? The answer is yes!

More importantly, you can heal yourself and others using these proven techniques. The first step is to understand that you can learn to *intentionally* direct your own energy fields or *electromagnetic fields* to help heal issues in yourself and others. Then get started with these 5 steps.

5 Steps to Feeling Your Own Energy Force

Step 1: In the world of metaphysics, intention is everything. First, have as quiet a mind as possible. With feet on the ground, barefoot if possible, take a deep breath in, hold it to a count of three, and release it slowly. Do this two more times.

---

69   See Lesley Graham's chapter 14.

Step 2: Taking in the next deep breath, place your hands at your feet and pull your hands physically up your legs, continuing by going up your torso, over your head, and then down each arm. You can do this a couple of times. This *touching* activates your meridians and chakras. Finish by rubbing your hands together, then cup your hands. (In the future when you do this exercise, you can visualize the process with the same effects very quickly.)

Step 3: While mentally focusing on your cupped hands, continue your deep breathing, focusing now on pulling a light of energy from above your head/crown and up from the ground/your feet. After imagining seeing this happen, gather the energy at heart level then push that energy stream into your hands.

Step 4: It's important to breathe deeply and focus on your hands during the process, so don't stop. Start pulling your hands apart slowly, followed by gently pushing them back together. Do this again several times with the distance between your hands increasing each time. Notice if there is any resistance pushing your hands back together. Close your eyes to really concentrate on the feeling between your hands. Does it tingle? Do you feel pressure? It's okay if you don't the first time; sometimes it takes time for this to develop.

Step 5: Once your hands feel resistance, you have experienced your own electromagnetic field. This is the healing energy used to shift blocked meridians, chakras, and more at the subatomic level. You can now place them somewhere you have physical pain. Once you feel the resistance between your hands, you will have experienced your own electromagnetic field. This is the healing energy you can use to shift blocked meridians, chakras, and more at the subatomic level. In other words, this is the energy you can use to heal yourself and others.

Next time you experience a pain in your body, follow steps 1–5 and then place your hands on the spot of the pain. Your may experience your whole body heat up. As you feel the heat, visualize the pain melting away. Your mind is stronger than your body, and when you get experienced enough at this, your body will respond. It will literally change the message it sends to your brain by releasing the flow and removing blocks.

It all begins by accepting that energy is real and that the study of how to use energy (quantum medicine) has been around a long time. For centuries, Hindu, Buddhist, and Egyptian medicine have used an extensive knowledge base of essential oils, stones, crystals, and herbs. We now know each has its own distinct vibration. By using that knowledge base we've discovered that the low *"illness"* vibration can be brought to a higher vibrancy. [70]

Use these techniques for someone you love and any blocks in the flow of energy will clear releasing the block or pain as they experience it. The more you practice on yourself and others, the faster you will feel the energy *shift* and the stronger the flow of energy will develop. Not only can you use electromagnetic energy transference on humans, you can also use it on animals and even plants.

Barbara Anne Cookson, a Certified Holistic Health Coach, says, *"Energy medicine is a powerful self-care tool for creating health and happiness."* [71]

Your body will learn when to stop intuitively, and the energy will be just the perfect amount to produce results. So the next time your child has a scraped knee, place your energized hands over the scrape and it will stop hurting and heal quickly.

Lorraine Pursell shares, *"Certainly this is why parents are so able to heal and help loved ones. When your child is hurting, your hand will*

---

70 If you've never had a chance to visit a sound chamber or a practitioner who uses crystal bowls, you really owe it to yourself to experience the soothing healing sounds from that experience.

71 See Barbara Anne Cookson's chapter 7.

almost always go to the afflicted area to soothe unless you cloud your intuition with self-doubt and logic." [72]

While this may seem strange to you, the fact is that most people regularly use the cupping technique in their daily lives without being aware they are doing it. We've used these techniques from childhood instinctively. Just hugging someone puts both energy fields together, providing energy exchange. In fact, teach this to your kids! I've found that kids love to learn to work with energy, so please pass this on to them. It may save someone's life (maybe even yours).

There are no mistakes in moving energy, so don't be afraid to try this. Your body will know exactly where these focused beams of energy from your hands need to go, so trust the technique and your body will show you what to do.

The more I've studied the vast number of modalities and techniques that science has discovered for us, the more excited I become about the gifts we all hold to heal ourselves and others. Even personal relationships within couples, families, or workplaces can be improved when you fully understand how to harness and use your energy.

As Barry Laub says, *"Opportunity often appears as adversity. The purpose of your life is usually revealed at times like this. Your adversity has driven your purpose in this lifetime."* [73]

There are checks and balances in the universe, and the laws of attraction, metaphysics, physics, chemistry, and more amaze me each and every day. I remind my clients on a regular basis that *sometimes the least thought or intention produces the most powerful result.* So use the 5 Steps I've outlined for you and discover the miracle of energy you hold in your hands.

KATERINA ST. CLAIRE is a retired Department of Homeland Security employee, certified as a top level first responder, and a member of the American Holistic Medical Association (AHMA). She helps people of all ages identify and use their unique healing

---

72   See Lorraine Pursell's chapter 11.
73   See Barry Laub's chapter 13.

skills so they can help save lives in cases of emergency. Learn more about Katerina in "Meet the Experts."

›16‹

HOW TO BE AN ENTREPRENEUR IN A 9 TO 5 JOB

Rose Sheehan, MBA

Mary, a mid-level corporate executive, sits in her office. She can't breathe! The feeling of suffocation overwhelms her as the four cubicle walls close in. She sits and stares through the computer screen, wondering if there is a way to escape the mundane, ineffective job she's felt stuck in for years. She's feeling exhausted and insignificant and drowning in her suppressed creativity, and the screams of frustration inside her head get louder as she works late into the evening to meet an extremely aggressive deadline but instead wants to be home with her family.

Mary would have been happier if she felt she was an entrepreneur employed by the company and working for herself. I know this, because that corporate executive was me, 15 years ago. I asked my colleagues and discovered I wasn't the only one that felt this way.

As part of my MBA studies I had created and conducted a workforce satisfaction survey and was shocked at the results! The most common feedback was:

- I don't enjoy what I'm doing.
- I don't feel appreciated.
- My work doesn't seem to have a purpose.
- There are no opportunities for growth.
- I don't have enough time to spend with my family.
- My boss keeps changing the priorities.
- I can't seem to stay focused.
- I'm exhausted!

If you are in human resources or are a business owner reading this article, do you understand that this kind of suffering is an epidemic?

The *New York Times* has reported that according to international research studies by Gallup, *Harvard Business Review*, and the Energy Project, low levels of employee satisfaction and morale and high levels of exhaustion and disengagement are very common whether you are male or female, a lower-level employee or a top executive; 87% of workers polled around the world fall into these categories![74]

Now I have worked with dozens of companies and hundreds of teams during my career. Not every individual I worked with or mentored viewed themselves as an entrepreneur. They didn't realize that their solutions were brilliant. Sometimes they didn't know how to present and implement their ideas, or even know that they filled a need. Do you?

One of my passions is to help corporate employees regain ownership of their stake in the company by reengaging as entrepreneurial employees. Let's face it: We are all by our very nature entrepreneurs! We have the ability to create the business life we want, whether you are an employee or an owner. "Entrepreneur" at its very

---

74 Tony Schwartz and Christine Porath, "Why You Hate Work," *New York Times*, May 30, 2014.

core is defined here as "someone who solves problems and is vested in the outcome."

Do you have a sense of ownership in everything you do? If not, what if you had the power to turn this around? I'll show you how you too can reconnect with your entrepreneurial spirit and bring it into the workplace.[75]

The exercises to follow are intended to help you, as a corporate employee, shift your mindset, because you actually do have a stake in the company.

The following exercises are an abbreviated version of a longer program from my workshops.

The "WOW" Epiphany

After hitting my low point and before I had the revelation of being an entrepreneur in a 9 to 5 job with an entrepreneurial stake in the company, these are questions I asked myself, sitting in that corporate office all those years ago.

W = What

What are the top concerns that prevent you from thriving as an entrepreneur in a 9 to 5 job? Write your list and think about how each item makes you feel.

_____.

_____.

_____.

_____.

_____.

O = Opposite

What would it look like if your environment was the opposite of the list you just created and these concerns were addressed? Look at the following example.

---

75   Rita Ferguson says, *"As a business owner of a small manufacturing company, I value the entrepreneurial employee."* See Rita Ferguson's chapter 6.

From my MBA employee satisfaction survey feedback list, I have created opposite statements here.

- I love what I am doing!
- I am loved and appreciated by all!
- My work has deep meaning and is impactful!
- There are endless opportunities!
- I have all the time I want to spend with my family!
- I have only one priority at a time!
- I am focused and clear on what I will do and how!
- I have endless energy!

Now write your opposite statements below.

1. _____.
2. _____.
3. _____.
4. _____.
5. _____.

W = Want

What perfect workplace features do you want? (HINT: You already created a list.) From your opposite statements above, you created a description of what you want. Knowing what you want is the first step in solving the problem of getting what you want.[76]

Finish by deciding what you will do to create or promote your perfect workplace environment.

How to "LAUNCH" for Success

Now that you have identified what you want; the question becomes *"How do I position myself to succeed as an entrepreneurial employee?"* If you recall, earlier in this chapter "entrepreneur" was defined as

---

76   Marilyn Ida Horowitz says, *"Writing is a basic form of self-communication. Any type of guided writing exercise will help you gain a fresh perspective and help you understand what you want. It is hard for us know what we want, but we always know what we don't want. The fast track to solving business problems is to write about how you feel."* See Marilyn Ida Horowitz's chapter 8.

"someone who solves problems and is vested in the outcome." Finish this section of the exercise to complete your entrepreneurial blueprint for success. These are questions I asked myself once I knew what I wanted and was ready to create my perfect workplace.

L = Love

What are you passionate about?

Are you passionate about what you do? If not, is it a means to get you to where you will do what you are passionate about?

If not, what you are doing is not sustainable and your chances of succeeding are slim.

A = Assess

What are you great at? Which of those things match with what you LOVE doing?

The quickest path to success is when you are doing what you already know well or can learn easily.

Here's how to build a business idea for your company or yourself. Get a pen and piece of paper. On the left side, list the top 5 things you EXCEL at doing in your career; on the right side of your page, list the top 5 things you LOVE doing most.

Now think back to a time when you were in school when you had to match words or ideas listed on the left side of the page to words or ideas on the right side of the page.

Find the best match for you!

U = Understand Your Gaps and Your Impact

What don't you know how to do?

List the things you don't know how to do and build a team to fill these gaps.

Include family or friends as part of your team to help you make decisions—particularly when the decisions affect them. Whether you are an employee, hold the executive office at a corporation, or are a business owner, the support of your family, friends, and associates has a direct impact on your success.[77]

N = Numbers

Do you know your numbers?

As an entrepreneur employee or a business owner, what resources do you have and what do you need?

Knowing this and being able to communicate clearly to those who can provide what you need (associate, boss, the executive office, contractor, lender, etc.) is important to your success.

C = Cause

What is it that you believe in?

What is your cause that is bigger than your own life? What values do you stand for? How does this relate to what you do in business?

Know this, and it will pull you through your challenges.

H = Have Fun

Are you having FUN?

It is more sustainable and invigorating if you love what you do, are great at doing it, are working with the best team and resources for you, are living with purpose, and are having fun!

The *New York Times* reported on a Gallup analysis of 263 research studies across 192 companies comparing the differences in company performance relative to employee involvement, passion, focus, energy, and enthusiasm. The analysis showed that the top quartile *"had 22% higher profitability, 10% higher customer ratings, 28% less theft, and 48% fewer safety incidents."*[78] This suggests that when employee needs are met, people thrive, families thrive, and companies thrive![79]

---

77 Joyce Sawyer says, *"When you are in business, your success will be enhanced if you consider ways to enroll your spouse for support."* See Joyce Sawyer's chapter 9.

78 Tony Schwartz and Christine Porath, "Why You Hate Work," *New York Times*, May 30, 2014.

79 Steven Sanchez says, *"In today's international, mobile phone– and social media–driven economy, the right choice for corporations is to embrace and empower entrepreneurship amongst their employees."* See Steven Sanchez's chapter 5.

One key question remains: Is it possible for corporations to create an ecosystem for entrepreneurship? The answer is yes (Facebook, Microsoft, Google, and others!) The more important question is: What ecosystem will you create for your own work life?

Each of us makes choices about where we work and how to thrive in this world. My perfect workplace is not perfect for everyone. However, it is one that balances my favorite features, as should yours.

Position yourself to be flexible. Understand your strengths, weaknesses, abilities, and desires. Ultimately it is YOUR choice to excel as an entrepreneurial employee in a 9 to 5 (or even as a business owner).

To recap: I've had the privilege of helping small, large, and multinational corporations grow their bottom line by leading and mentoring thousands of individuals and helping them engage as entrepreneurs. By far the most effective way to solve problems or achieve goals is harnessing the energy of the entrepreneurial spirits.

What is one brilliant idea you have that will solve a simple challenge or fill a need at your company or in your business? Write it down:

_____

Now use the exercises above to map out your entrepreneurial blueprint to launch your idea successfully!

ROSE SHEEHAN, MBA, is a philanthropist, business owner, business mentor, speaker, and number one international bestselling author. She spent more than two decades in the corporate world managing high-performance teams for corporations such as the US-based Merck & Co. and Merck KGaA, Darmstadt. She is the founder of Golden Egg Global and ATKC LLC. Learn more about Rose in "Meet the Experts."

CONGRATULATIONS!

You've finished reading!
So much information . . .
Where do you begin?

First, turn the page and "Meet the Experts." Get to know the very real people who have shared their hearts and strategies with you.

Then, go back to the beginning of this book and start again!

Begin with the preface and complete the two charts for your business and life.

Then, one by one, review each chapter and gradually incorporate the Expert Success Solution into your business and your life.

Remember: Success only comes with implementation. Start now and don't ever stop until you have everything you want—in your business and your life!

MEET THE EXPERTS

Wendy Lipton-Dibner, MA

WENDY LIPTON-DIBNER, MA, is a multiple-time bestselling author and internationally recognized authority in business acceleration through impact strategy. As president of Professional Impact, Inc. and founder of *The Action Movement*™, her unique strategies have helped clients increase revenues exponentially in record time by making an impact on every life they touch.

Wendy received her master's degree in sociology and social psychology from Duke University and was recruited for a position as a university instructor and director of organizational research studies. One of her projects caught the eye of the United States Senate, where her presentation influenced a decision that has since helped millions of people.

Driven to make a lasting impact on people's lives, Wendy left academia to open her first business: a social laboratory to develop and test formulas to move people to action. Within three months, her retail and service sales skyrocketed beyond industry standards and she became a sought-after consultant for small businesses, sharing the formulas she'd discovered for sales, leadership, and customer service.

Wendy went on to get certified in three schools of psychology and built a private practice specializing in sales professionals. Her proprietary blend of psychotherapy and sales and leadership training helped her clients dramatically increase revenues and led to a swell of invitations for consulting and training for Fortune 100 organizations, where she became known for creating solid results in record time.

Since then, Wendy has served as a trusted advisor and coach to doctors, executives, entrepreneurs, and top influencers, delivering thousands of customized training and consulting programs in health care, Fortune 100 businesses, small businesses, and nonprofit organizations. She is a sought-after media guest and keynote speaker, and her bestselling books are required reading at businesses and in medical and dental schools. Known as a "world-class speaker," she's touched millions of lives around the globe, and her *Move People to Action*™ live event and e-course have been named *"the most comprehensive training ever created for impact-driven entrepreneurs."*

Visit Wendy at www.ProfessionalImpact.com, and be sure to visit www.TheActionMovement.com for complimentary training videos to help you grow your impact, influence, and income.

Rick Frishman

RICK FRISHMAN is a publisher at Morgan James Publishing in New York and founder of Planned Television Arts (now called Media Connect). He has been one of the leading book publicists in America for over 37 years. Rick works with many of the top book editors, literary agents, and publishers in America, including Simon and Schuster, HarperCollins, and Random House. He has worked with bestselling authors such as Mitch Albom, Bill Moyers, Stephen King, Caroline Kennedy, Howard Stern, President Jimmy Carter, Sophia Loren, Smokey Robinson, Nelson DeMille, Salman Rushdie, John Grisham, Yogi Berra, Henry Kissinger, Jack Canfield, Alan Dershowitz, Arnold Palmer, Jackie Collins, Whoopi Goldberg, Governor Mario Cuomo, and Senator John Glenn.

Morgan James Publishing publishes fiction and nonfiction books by authors with a platform who believe in giving back. Morgan James gives a portion of the proceeds of every book sold to Habitat for Humanity. Rick has also appeared on hundreds of radio shows and more than a dozen TV shows nationwide, including *Oprah*, and on Fox News and Bloomberg TV. He has also been featured in the *New York Times*, the *Wall Street Journal*, Associated Press stories, *Selling Power* magazine, the *New York Post*, and scores of other publications. He has appeared on stage with notables such as Sir Richard Branson, the Dalai Lama, T. Harv Eker, Jack Canfield, Mark Victor Hansen, Tony Hsieh, David Bach, Brian Tracy, Zig Ziglar, and Brendon Burchard.

Rick is the co-author of 16 books, including national bestsellers *Guerrilla Publicity*, *Where's Your Wow*, *Guerrilla Marketing for Writers*, *The Expert Success Solution*, and *250 Rules of Business*. Rick's 15th book,

Networking Magic, Second Edition was published in January 2014. *Author 101: The Insider's Guide to Publishing* is Rick's 16th book. Rick has a BFA in acting and directing and a BS in communications from Ithaca College. He is a sought-after lecturer on publishing and public relations and a member of the Public Relations Society of America and the National Speakers Association. Rick and his wife, Robbi, live in Long Island, New York, with their two Havanese puppies, Cody and Cooper. They have three children: Adam, Rachel, and Stephanie.

Go to www.RickFrishman.com for more information and get Rick's Million Dollar Rolodex.

Pat Skiffington

PAT SKIFFINGTON is an entrepreneur, author, coach, and internationally recognized business expert and sales leader. He is a highly sought-after speaker whose keynotes are known for being content-rich, dynamic, and inspirational. In 2006, Pat was inducted into the National Speakers Association. He is also a consultant who is frequently called upon by businesses looking to grow their profitability and increase their market share.

Pat brings more than three decades of experience as a successful entrepreneur and corporate executive to his work. He is a former senior executive of a Fortune 50 company, winning multiple awards for his leadership in both sales and operations. At one point in his career, Pat was responsible for the sales activities of more than 900 salespeople. He is also an innovative, results-driven, and highly sought-after sales trainer. In 2014, he became the managing partner of Grimes & Associates in Oklahoma City, a sales training company that has trained hundreds of thousands of financial services sales associates over the last 38 years.

First and foremost, Pat is an entrepreneur and owns 10 successful and profitable companies, including the Keller Williams Classic Realty Group in Orlando, Florida, consisting of five franchised real estate offices employing more than 450 independent sales associates. Pat is recognized by Inman News as one of the top 500 power brokers in North America and has been featured in the *Wall Street Journal*, *U.S. News and World Report*, *Bloomberg Businessweek*, and Reuters stories, and on BBC Radio. **Get your free training video to help you Master the Seven Pillars at www.TheSevenPillars.com.**

Helena Nyman

HELENA NYMAN is an expert on high performance with a passion for helping people unlock their full potential and reach their peak performance. Her clients have included the top 1% in sports, politics, and business in more than 40 countries, including the president of a European nation and royalty.

Prior to starting her executive consulting company, Helena coached world-class and Olympic athletes. For 15 years, Helena has served as president of Nyman Consulting International, and she is the founder and president of the Executive Center of Excellence, bringing her sports experience to the business community and helping her clients grow their businesses by striving for the gold.

In 2009, Helena was a global Artemis Award honoree and was inducted into the Women's Hall of Fame. In 2013, she received the National Academy of Bestselling Authors Award. As a keynote speaker and philanthropist, she spreads her message of peak performance around the world.

To learn more about how to perform at the gold level, visit Helena at www.HelenaNyman.com, and for two special gifts to help you capture the gold, visit www.IHateMySilverMedal.com.

Steven Sanchez

STEVEN SANCHEZ creates custom Internet business plans and solutions for industry-leading businesses and individuals. The company he founded in 1992 has grown up alongside today's commercial Internet. For more than 20 years he has designed and built sophisticated systems for everything from cruise lines and racing companies to small medical practices and even home-based businesses.

Steven not only designs solutions that are tailored to a company's particular goals and objectives, he also helps those companies integrate those solutions with their current level of operations. Steven has personally evaluated and implemented hundreds of unique programs and services, as well as trained clients and staff to effectively use them to grow their businesses. This experience makes Steven especially qualified to sort through the wide range of choices available today to come up with just the right solution for your particular needs.

Steven lives in Los Angeles with his wife and four children. When he's not working on the Internet, he enjoys writing, watching movies, sailing, scuba diving, and getting together with friends.

If you would like to reach Steven about developing your own customized Internet success plan, visit MyCustomPlan.com and be sure to download your free Website Success Sequence Checklist at www.MyCustomPlan.com/expert.

Rita Ferguson

RITA FERGUSON is an expert in business planning and the application of project management techniques to meet organizational objectives while increasing implementation speed and reducing cost.

After graduating with a BA in economics, Rita pursued a career with Fortune 500 companies, managing diverse segments of business operations in the areas of finance, sales, logistics, customer service, and project management.

When working for a global chemical company that suffered a tragic plant explosion, Rita, then the customer service manager, became an integral member of the crisis leadership team responsible for successfully rebuilding the business unit. That event sparked her passion in project management and she became a certified Project Management Professional (PMP).

To effectively meet the challenges of the ever-changing business environment, Rita earned a black belt in Lean Sigma, achieving expert status in business process improvement. Additionally, she became a certified facilitator in root cause investigation, opportunity analysis, and risk assessment.

Today, Rita is actively involved in her family's business. As a third-generation owner, she applies her in-the-trenches knowledge and experience to the challenge of running a small manufacturing operation in today's vibrant economy.

Rita is a speaker, corporate trainer, and certified High Performance Coach. She speaks on topics of strategic thinking and project alignment to achieve short- and long-term business goals.

Connect with Rita at www.BusinessGoalAchievement.com.

Barbara Anne Cookson, LMT, CHC

BARBARA ANNE COOKSON, LMT, CHC, spent 23 years in dentistry before she changed direction to become a licensed massage therapist and group fitness instructor. As Barbara's clients watched her get happier and healthier, they started asking for help reaching their own goals.

Barbara cared for her father through years of debilitating illness, and then for a dear friend through her journey and death with cancer. That was when Barbara realized her mission is to help people remember their innate power to create their own health and happiness. She became certified as a Holistic Health Coach and now works with clients to empower them to reach their own peak health and happiness.

In addition to being a sought-after presenter and speaker, Barbara has written for *Massage Magazine* and is a contributing author for the popular blog NotYourMothersMenopause.com. She has created training programs for workplace and corporate wellness to create a healthy, happy, and less stressed work environment for employees *(and the boss!)*.

Barbara's energy, enthusiasm, and style engages, inspires, and motivates audiences. She shares her message of happy, healthy being in online videos and live events and workshops.

To learn more about Barbara and receive your free, five-video workshop to help you navigate the Circle of Happy and Healthy, visit www.TheCircleOfHappyAndHealthy.com.

Marilyn Ida Horowitz

MARILYN IDA HOROWITZ is an award-winning New York University professor, author, producer, and Manhattan-based writing coach who works with successful novelists, produced screenwriters, and award-winning filmmakers.

She completed her tenure as a judge for the Fulbright Program for film and media students. In 2004 she received the coveted New York University Award for Teaching Excellence.

Professor Horowitz is the force behind a revolutionary system that yields a new, more effective way of writing. She is the author of six books that help the writer learn her trademarked system, including editions for college, high school, and middle school.

She is featured in the *Now Write! Screenwriting* anthology, edited by Sherry Ellis and published by Tarcher/Penguin.

Marilyn's upcoming suspense thriller, *The Book of Zev*, will be out in December 2014.

Professor Horowitz has taught more than 100 classes, seminars, and workshops across the country for groups including the Writers Guild of America East and the Philadelphia Writer's Conference.

Professor Horowitz has written several feature-length screenplays. Her production credits include the feature film *And Then Came Love* (2007), starring Vanessa Williams and distributed by Warner Bros.

To learn more about Professor Horowitz, sign up for either of her newsletters, or claim your free Formative Event Template, enter code FORMFREE at www.marilynhorowitz.com/resources/.

Joyce Sawyer

JOYCE SAWYER is a long-standing political spouse who supported her husband, Tom Sawyer (his real name!), in more than 30 elections since 1976. She has been in the public eye throughout her husband's career at all three levels of political service:

- National—in Congress
- State—in the House of Representatives, the Senate, and the board of education
- Local—as the mayor of Akron, Ohio

Joyce served as a middle and high school teacher for 30 years and spent decades serving as a political spouse. She contends that being a spouse is "the hardest job in American politics."

In her groundbreaking book, *Power Spousing* (foreword by Senator John Glenn and Mrs. Annie Glenn), Joyce offers advice, insight, and encouragement to all spouses who are working hard to make someone else look good while maintaining their own identity along the way.

Joyce serves as a coach to power spouses and loves helping all spouses who have been stifled in the spotlight. Her powerful advice extends beyond the political sphere to all high-profile fields, including business, medicine, the ministry, and the military.

Although Joyce is a native of New Jersey, her many "adventures with Tom Sawyer" have taken place in their home state of Ohio, as well as in Washington, where Joyce has thrived in the spotlight, been trained in mediation, and stayed active in her community. **For advice and guidance to make sure you don't get Stifled in the Spotlight, go to www.StifledintheSpotlight.com for a complimentary video message from Joyce.**

Ann Van De Water

ANN VAN DE WATER is a wife, mother, and now a grandmother. As a Certified Leadership Parenting Coach, through speaking, coaching, and writing she is dedicated to helping parents, and specifically moms, thrive—not just survive—their journey by offering Stress-Less Parenting strategies and tips. She loves being a mom and is passionate about parenting.

Ann coaches couples who are facing challenges in their childrearing to bring peace into their homes, and she believes there are ways to foster communication and engage young adults, especially during the teen years. She offers practical advice and reachable goals to her clients as a coach who cares!

Ann is also the published author of *Mommy Memoirs,* a humorous Morgan James publication in which she reminds us that laughter and a sense of humor heal and can get us through the toughest days. Her greatest joy is sharing her wisdom, experiences, and positive outlook with mothers of all ages as a sought-after speaker. She has proven that a happy, healthy home and Stress-Less Parenting can come true!

Contact Ann at www.AnnVanDeWater.com for more information and to download her free gift to you: the audio file "10 Tips for Lowering Your Stress as You Raise Your Rugrats!"

Lorraine Pursell, MA

LORRAINE PURSELL, MA, has been guiding individuals, couples, and families into personal peace and loving relationships through private practice, radio, speaking, video, and writing since 1995. Her own journey from depression to personal power is the source of her inspiring, approachable style, which is well received by clients and audiences everywhere.

Lorraine specializes in one-on-one private retreats where people can transform beyond their frustrations into the happy lives and loving relationships they want. Her humorous, nonjudgmental coaching manner helps facilitate lasting change. Her passion is helping people feel good.

Lorraine is the author of *Affirmations for Kids and Parents* CDs and books, *The 12 Secrets for Safe, Happy, and Confident Kids,* and *The Women's Self-Love Journey* coaching programs. Her popular column, "A Positive Mental Note," appears weekly in the *Williston Herald.* Lorraine holds a counseling master's degree and educational therapist board certification, and has practiced in California, Hawai'i, and now in North Dakota, where she lives with her son and his family.

For more information and to subscribe to Lorraine's uplifting videos, quotes, and tips on happy living and peaceful families, visit www.LorrainePursell.com. Get Lorraine's free, informative e-book *Stop Yelling at Your Kids: 3 Foolproof Ways to Keep Your Cool* at *www.StopYellingAtYourKids.com.*

Angela Alexander

ANGELA ALEXANDER is dedicated to helping others search for their miracles through her book *Miracles in Action,* the associated workbook, and her speaking engagements.

On April Fool's Day 2000, while Angela was in Japan on military duty, her two eight-year-old sons, Murice and Roger, died instantly in a horrific car crash. The miracle is that God allowed both of her sons to write and leave behind incredible good-bye letters.

Angela said, "Each letter answered specific questions that I would have wondered about for the rest of my life." As a result, in 2005 Angela retired from the Air Force and is now an inspirational speaker and author of her autobiography, titled *Miracles in Action: Turning Pain into Power and Grief into Peace.*

A documentary film is currently in production about Angela's amazing story. She's a sought-after speaker and shares this amazing testimony at churches, conferences, retreats, book clubs, and women's fellowships.

Angela has been a guest on many secular and Christian television and radio talk shows and has spoken on missionary trips in Nairobi, Belize, and Trinidad.

To order *Miracles in Action* or to invite Angela to speak at your event, please visit www.MiraclesInAction.com.

Barry Laub, MS, CFP

BARRY LAUB, MS, CFP, is a number one bestselling author and the president of Infinite Resources, Inc., a consulting, training, and coaching company. He is known for transforming businesses, careers, and lives. Barry is a highly sought-after and engaging speaker.

A recent client testimonial described Barry as having "a real gift for helping his clients work on the key intangibles that benefit them professionally and personally. Through our work together in these recent months, he has provided me with the tools and foundational work to 're-engineer' my mindset, resulting in vastly more self-confidence, assurance, and savviness to deal with important business discussions and everyday situations. I can think of no book, lecture, or other teaching venue that could have been more effective."

Barry received his master's degree in guidance and counseling and special education. He had a distinguished career as a program director, guidance counselor, and teacher trainer for the New York City Board of Education. After leaving the field of education, Barry received recognition as a top producing financial planner, especially in helping families that have members with special needs.

After his successful career in education, he created a national employee benefits company, where he served as CEO for more than 40 employees.

Utilizing these experiences, Barry maintains a private coaching and speaking practice. He conducts mastermind groups and teleseminars, is a radio personality, and has been interviewed on many television shows. His target market is primarily business owners, sales professionals, and business executives.

Barry is a results-oriented coach with the ability to put his clients at ease while maintaining accountability. He is an active Rotarian, serving as faculty member of the Rotary Leadership Institute and active with Rotary Youth Leadership.

Barry's passion is using his experience to create environments which support others to live a gratifying and satisfying life. He is the proud and joyous grandfather of eight grandchildren.

Visit Barry at www.GratefulandSatisfied.com.

Lesley Graham, RN

LESLEY GRAHAM, RN, is a specialist nurse, coach, Reiki master, and founder of Stand Up and Take Charge, where she offers advice, inspirational stories, and alternative ways of healing as well as the truth about what the doctors don't tell you.

Lesley's passion is to help people recognize and utilize their innate ability to self-heal physically, psychologically and spiritually.

Having completed her coaching diploma in 2009, she has worked closely with human resources coaching staff on the Improving Working Lives Initiative.

While working in public health, Lesley developed and delivered a new training program using social marketing principles to engage pregnant mothers to stop smoking. After hitting targets in record time, she was awarded the Innovation for Success Award, providing numerous seminars to consultants, doctors, nurses, and midwives.

Lesley retired in 2012 due to ill health after being bitten by a tick in Ireland. Having now made a remarkable recovery, she shares her story to empower women and those with chronic illness.

For Lesley's free brochure "What the Doctors Don't Tell You," visit her website at www.StandUpAndTakeCharge.com.

▶ Katerina St. Claire ◀

KATERINA ST. CLAIRE is an author, speaker, integrative medicine practitioner, certified tutor, and substitute schoolteacher. She is also a member of the American Holistic Medical Association.

After facing a debilitating illness the medical community couldn't reverse, Katerina decided to take matters into her own hands. After a thorough Internet search of creditable alternative medicine practices, Healing Beyond Borders was her first choice. Katerina loved the work so much that she attained a level 4 certification before starting her Quantum-Touch certificate program.

Today, Katerina is a Certified Quantum-Touch Practitioner and is working toward her PhD in integrative medicine at the International Quantum University of Integrative Medicine. She has studied color and sound therapy in addition to other modalities too numerous to mention.

Katerina has taken her background in homeland security and combined it with alternative medicine techniques to produce a unique teaching program for people of all ages.

Her *gifts* are a very strong electromagnetic field and her intuition, which were greatly enhanced after her near-death experience at age 21. She uses these gifts daily in her practice and at her church. Katerina also loves working with animals.

Visit Katerina at www.MiracleAdvantage.com/freegift for your free MP3 grounding meditation and book.

Rose Sheehan, MBA

ROSE SHEEHAN, MBA, is a philanthropist, business owner, business mentor, investor, world traveler, speaker, and number one international bestselling author. In 2014, she was honored by the Bestselling Authors International Organization.

Rose spent more than two decades in the corporate world managing high-performance teams for corporations such as the US-based Merck & Co.; Merck KGaA, Darmstadt (formerly LIPHA Pharmaceuticals/Dey LP); Chiron Corporation; and Robert E. Lamb, Inc.

She is an executive business advisor and mentor for Powerteam International; Diamond Executive Services, Inc.; Mo'Movers LLC; and many others. She has led and mentored thousands of individuals within these and other companies.

Rose earned her MBA from Golden Gate University, specializing in corporate management and international business. She is the founder of Golden Egg Global and ATKC LLC, focused on helping people and businesses thrive through her Golden Success workshop series and programs.

A portion of all Rose's business revenues fund programs such as the Pathway Home PTSD Veterans' Program and the Boys' and Girls' Clubs of America.

For a free one-on-one evaluation session with Rose, go to www.HappyInA9to5.com and submit your results from the chapter questionnaire!

CONNECT WITH THE EXPERTS!

Join us on our Facebook page and get ongoing success tips from our experts!

We look forward to meeting you in our Facebook Community!